Put a CAP On It!

Practical Reading For:
- Singles
- Significant Others
- Pre-Marital Couples
- Married Couples
- Anyone interested in marriage

Alfred T. Lands

Copyright © 2024 **Alfred T. Lands**

All rights reserved. No part of this publication may be reproduced, distributed, or transmitted in any form or by any means, including photocopying, recording, or other electronic or mechanical methods, without the prior written permission of the publisher, except in the case of brief quotations embodied in critical reviews and certain other noncommercial uses permitted by copyright law. For permission requests, write to the publisher, addressed "Attention: Book Rights and Permission," at the address below.

Published in the United States of America

ISBN 978-1-962730-90-7 (SC)
ISBN 978-1-962730-89-1 (HC)
ISBN 978-1-962730-68-6 (Ebook)

Alfred T. Lands
9384 Windy Ct
Jonesboro, GA 30238
alfredtlands@gmail.com

Ordering Information and Rights Permission:

Quantity sales. Special discounts might be available on quantity purchases by corporations, associations, and others. For details, contact the publisher at the address above.

For Book Rights Adaptation and other Rights Permission. Call us at toll-free 404-964-4639 or send us an email at alfredtlands@gmail.com.

Dedication

This first writing is dedicated to my bride of 41 years, Bishop Reverend Rosemary Lands. We discovered the truths written in this book together. Through love, commitment, and collaboration, this first formal writing on family was born. It has been our calling and lifetime journey "to take the family to godly heights" together.

To our daughters, Trunae Alyse "Big Tru" Green and Trulyse Faith "Lil Tru" Lands, who have honored us as their parents since birth. To all of the other family members, which includes our son, Thomas Green (Trunae's husband), "the Green beans," Tylan, Tory, and Tyla; our son Pastor Darien & Minister Shakiera Brooks; "the Brooklings", Darien Jr., Donovan, Destin, Dasia, and Dawson; and our son Pastor Taj B. Lands, for allowing us to make a small contribution in their lives.

To Guiding Light Baptist Church, Greater Cavalry Bible Church, Union Grove Baptist Church, Mount Hermon Baptist Church, New Calvary Missionary Baptist Church, The Greater Piney Grove Baptist Church, and Family Life Missionary Baptist Church for trusting us as we developed and modeled the family-focused vision God has given us for this culture.

In conclusion, this book is a tribute to the one who made the ultimate sacrifice, saving us all so that we may fulfill His divine purpose—the one we adore as our Lord and Savior, Jesus Christ!

Foreword

It is with immense joy and gratitude that I introduce you to this remarkable book on marriage, authored by my beloved husband of 41 years. As a Pastor, a loving husband, and a father of three daughters, three sons, and a grandfather of six boys and two girls, he has not only committed his life to serving our congregation. Still, he has also poured his heart and wisdom into nurturing our marriage.

In a world where the institution of marriage can sometimes seem fragile and uncertain, this book serves as a beacon of hope and guidance. It is a testament to the enduring power of love, faith, and unwavering commitment. Through the pages of this book, you will embark on a journey—a journey that explores the depths of what it means to truly love and cherish your spouse, for richer or poorer, in sickness and in health, till death do us part. It is a reminder that marriage is God's design.

My husband's insights are not just abstract; they are born from the gut of real-life experiences. He has witnessed the joys and challenges of countless couples within our congregation and has walked alongside them, offering solace, counsel, and unwavering support. His wisdom has been honed through years of helping others navigate the intricate path of marriage, and now he shares these profound lessons with you.

This book is not just a summary of marital advice; it is a heartfelt testament to the beauty of a marriage founded on faith, trust, and love in God. As I read the words he has carefully laid out, I am reminded of our countless moments—moments of laughter, tears, and unshakable unity. I see our love story reflected in these pages, and I am grateful for the life we have built together.

In the following chapters, you will discover invaluable insights into communication, conflict resolution, intimacy, and so much more. You will be inspired to foster a marriage that is not just enduring but thriving—a marriage that brings you closer to your spouse and closer to God.

Alfred T. Lands

As you embark on this journey through the wisdom and experience of my husband, may you find renewed hope, strengthened resolve, and a deeper appreciation for the sacred bond of marriage. May your marriage be enriched and blessed through the lessons shared in these pages.

Love Forever,

Your Bride, Bishop Rev. Rosemary Lands, MSW, M.Div.

Contents

Dedication iii
Foreword iv
Introduction viii
Chapter 1: - God's Design For Two People In A Covenantal Relationship ... 1
1. Biblical Model for Marriage 5
2. Accountability Element 7
Finances 9
Relationships 9
Decisions 10
Technology 11
3. A God-Directed Marriage 12
Chapter 2: - Learn It, Live It 13
1. Pay Attention 13
2. Commit to Learning 14
3. Refresh 15
Chapter 3: Sunup to Sundown 17
1. Get Up in Your Commitment 18
2. Walk Out in Your Marriage 19
3. Lay Down and Start 21
Chapter 4: - I Can Do Five 22
1. Somebody Needs to Make up That Bed 24
2. Home Cooking 27
3. We Are in It for the Long Haul 29
Chapter 5: Feeding a Hungry Marriage 32
1. Appetizer 35
2. Main course 36
3. Desert 37
Chapter 6: Say So 41

1. A Husband's Position in His Marriage Is the Leader! 41
2. A Wife's Position in the Marriage 44
3. The Creator's Position 47

Chapter 7: - The Telling Three T's 50
1. Tripping 50
2. Treatment 51
3. Trusting 52

Chapter 8: - Where Are We Now? 54
1. No More Disagreements 54
2. Who Is Living in This House? 58
3. A New Car 59

Chapter 9: - Marriage On Automatic 60
1. Driving with One Hand on the Wheel 61
2. Distractions Without Disruptions 61
3. Spouse Forever 63

Chapter 10: - The Display 65
1. Seen On Purpose 68
2. Being Seen Unaware 69
3. Change the View 70

Chapter 11: - Gaining While Maintaining 72
1. Intentional Acts of Kindness 72
2. Marriage Development 73
3. A Tighter Connection 74

Chapter 12: - Capping It Off! 76
1. Greatest Investment Ever 76
2. The Best Quality of Life 77
3. The Oneness 79

Appendix 81
A Brief Look at the Author 89

Introduction

What is the difference between a man and a woman? First, God made man and woman unique, uniquely different.

For many, marriage is a daunting quest. A journey with no clear path. A fight with no clear winner. However, marriage is as simple for many as 1, 2, 3... Some unions have accepted the biblical model. Also, today, some marriages pattern themselves after biblical examples. These marriages can be misleading. They are nestled with many issues between the man and the woman that ultimately show themselves throughout that union's life.

Some marriages are operating as God intended them to operate. In these marriages, the man understands his role, and the woman understands her position. Together, they can work a marriage that is pleasing to God.

Based on the biblical record in Genesis chapter 2, every marriage has an opportunity to be successful. Unfortunately, many marriages will never experience what God intended for them because they will not take the time to learn what God has said about the model He created for marriage—A man will leave his mother and father and cleave to his wife, and they shall become one flesh.

When we look closely at what the Scripture says about marriage, we can detect the plan and God's marriage process. The married couple, specifically the man, is given full responsibility for his marriage from the very beginning. He must be willing to take his family to a place where God can begin to weave them together for them to become one flesh. He must be willing to link up with someone he doesn't know, as well as his mother and father. He must have the courage to put his whole trust and faith in an invisible God.

Alfred T. Lands

Chapter 1:
God's Design For Two People In A Covenantal Relationship

Coronavirus: COVID-19 Pandemic Can't Stop Man's Love for His Ailing Wife[1]

MANSFIELD - Call it love in the time of the coronavirus pandemic.

Ophinell Davis, 88, can't visit his wife, Mildred, because of the threat of COVID-19. Mildred, a Liberty Nursing Center of Mansfield resident, has developed dementia.

But that doesn't prevent Ophinell from being present in Mildred's life. He still stops by the nursing home, usually twice daily, to stand outside her window.

"Sometimes, she recognizes me. Sometimes she doesn't," Ophinell said.

He often leaves snacks on the porch for his beloved Mildred. They had been married for sixty-eight years on June 9.

Diana Johnson, a life enrichment coordinator for Liberty Nursing Center, gets choked up when she thinks of the couple's love story.

"He is the poster boy of dedication," Johnson said of Ophinell. "Every young person should witness the devotion he has to his wife. He needs to be part of the educational system."

Ophinell realized in the last couple of years that something was wrong with Mildred. She sometimes wet herself on the drive to the VA clinic in Cleveland.

"She started leaving the water run," he added.

One incident told him things would never be the same.

---

[1] Caudill, M. (2020, April 17, 2020). "Coronavirus: COVID-19 Pandemic can't stop man's love for his ailing wife." from https://www.mansfieldnewsjournal.com/story/news/2020/04/17/coronavirus-covid-19-pandemic-cant-stop-mans-love-wife/5143887002/.

Mildred was cooking for the grandchildren, insisting they were at the house when they weren't. All are adults.

"I sat on the steps and cried like a baby," Ophinell said. "I knew what was coming."

In late 2017, he knew he couldn't give Mildred the care she needed after she wandered out into the street. City firefighters brought her home.

"I still wanted to hold off, but I knew it was time," Ophinell said. "I couldn't wait any longer."

The love story begins.

Mildred came to Mansfield from Jasper, Alabama, after graduating high school in 1951. She stayed with her sister and helped raise her sister's two young boys.

The couple started dating in the fall of that year.

"I had to pass by her house on my way home," Ophinell said. "I thought I could never get enough of this woman."

When asked what he liked about Mildred, he said simply, "Everything."

Sitting in a recliner in the living room of their one-story, green and brown house on the city's south side, Ophinell recalled his courtship with his wife. He sat with a U.S. Marines blanket — a gift from the nursing home — draped over his legs.

"I didn't know what to say to a girl when I was eighteen," he said.

The young adult must have done something right. Ophinell and Mildred married on June 9, 1952, her 19th birthday.

"What she got was a ball of clay with a handful of work and not much time to do it," Ophinell said.

He was called to serve in the US Army during the Korean War. They were apart for two years while Ophinell served stateside.

"We went to a gypsy on Main Street," he said. "She told us I would be going on a long trip."

After his stint in the Army, Ophinell and Mildred were always together except for two weeks a year for his summer service in the Army Reserves.

Through the years Ophinell graduated from Mansfield Senior High School in 1951. While there, he was a standout athlete, helping the shuttle hurdle relay team to a record at the time.

He said he grew up poor.

"I didn't know what was on the other side of Bowman Street," he said.

As an adult, Ophinell worked security for forty years at leading businesses such as Westinghouse, Mansfield Tire, and Armco Corp. He also did ten years of security work at the local hospital.

Mildred worked the elevator at Richland Trust and met President John F. Kennedy when he came to town.

"She has an autograph of his," Ophinell said. "I don't know what happened to it."

Ophinell became a history buff. He has several displays throughout town detailing the history of the steel mill and Mansfield Senior football.

The Tigers won a state championship in 1949.

"It was just like the end of the Second World War," Ophinell said. "Everybody was uptown celebrating."

He and Mildred settled into small-town life.

"We had our ups and downs like everybody," Ophinell said. "She had to look the other way sometimes when I got in trouble."

Growing up in the church, Mildred became an usher at Mt. Calvary Baptist Church. She wouldn't miss a service and loved to garden.

They had one son, Dexter, who died ten years ago at fifty-five.

Their first home was on Prescott Street, near a railroad track. A family member gave Ophinell the lot. Ophinell said one of his friends noted,

"You always feel like you're going someplace" when visiting the house because of the frequent train traffic.

Mildred was eager to leave the noise, and the couple moved to Home Avenue for ten years before finding their permanent home on Dale Avenue in 1975.

"He hasn't had a woman's touch in two years," Ophinell lamented.

Life today Ophinell credits the couple's long lives to taking care of themselves. He and the late Mansfield police Chief Lawrence Harper were jogging partners while Mildred and a friend walked several miles daily.

"Take care of yourself when you're younger," Ophinell advised. "I was a physical specimen."

He knows the couple's time together is coming to an end and has already made arrangements.

"She was just a loving person. Everybody that ever met her liked her," Ophinell said of Mildred. "She was a forgiving person. She didn't hold any grudge against anybody."

"She was everything to me."

That's been evident to the staff at Liberty Nursing Center.

"I've made him a promise that she does not forget him as long as I'm here, and I can talk about Ophinell," Johnson said. "I have never witnessed anything like it in my life. I think they broke the mold."

Ophinell fondly recalled a day when the staff brought Mildred to the window and placed her hand against it when she saw him. He said he almost cried.

"I don't know if I'll see her again," he said.

Johnson is hopeful he will and that life will return to normal after the pandemic.

"As soon as this is over, we will throw a big party for Mr. Davis and Millie," she said.

We know that marriage is God's idea, and He designed it as a perfect fit for two individuals. To engage in God's design, they had to meet specific qualifications, male and female. God intended for His model to be occupied by a man and a woman. Let us examine some critical biblical truths about marriage.

1. Biblical Model for Marriage

"The Bible's statements on sexuality cannot be limited to the six main verses which condemn homosexuality. God created humans, male and female (specifically, He created a man and a woman, Adam and Eve) in the creation account. This sexual duality is central to human beings and the foundation for marriage. Thus, the monogamous, lifelong marriage is always the ideal in Scripture. While the Bible has numerous examples of positive portrayals of non-sexual love between two men or two women (Jonathan and David, or Ruth and Naomi, etc.), there is no positive portrayal of a homosexual relationship or hint of even the concept of homosexual marriage."[2]

He did not leave room for alternates or substitutes. The original idea for marriage had to do with Genesis 1:28.

Genesis 1:28 King James Version (KJV) 28 And God blessed them, and God said unto them, be fruitful, and multiply, and replenish the earth, and subdue it: and have dominion over the fish of the sea, and over the fowl of the air, and over every living thing that moved upon the earth.

"By seeing the word 'replenish,' people think (not surprisingly), 'Isn't God telling us that He wants Adam and Eve to refill the world?' And doesn't that mean it had previously been filled, then emptied?"[3]

"But as any Hebrew Interlinear Bible or Bible dictionary tells you, the word translated as 'replenish' in Genesis 1:28 is the Hebrew verb מלאו (mil'û), which means fill, not refill. Many modern versions translate the word in Genesis 1:28 as fill. But this does not necessarily mean the King James translators made a mistake here. They seem to have known what the Hebrew word meant, as shown by the fact that it appears in the Old Testament in most other places; they translated it as 'fill.'

---

[2] International, C. M. (2016). "Does the Bible condemn homosexuality?". from https://creation.com/does-the-bible-condemn-homosexuality.

[3] International, C. M. (2011). "Genesis 1:28 - Replenish or Fill." from http://creation.com/genesis-1-28-replenish-or-fill.

The key to unraveling the apparent confusion is that languages continually change. The usage of this word has changed since the KJV appeared some four hundred years ago (1611). Back then, people were more likely than nowadays to say things like 'I am replete with happiness,' which is another way of saying 'I am full of happiness.' And replenish (fill) is the verb form of the adjective replete (full). In earlier times, people reading the KJV would have likely understood replenish to mean precisely what the Hebrew word means, i.e., fill."

Now that we know what God said about the married couple's first responsibility, we should be ready to understand the model He created for marriage. God was and never will be confused about the relationship He established for a male and female. Regardless of what married people may do, God expects the married couple to maintain His original idea.

Let me be explicitly clear. A God-honored marriage is between one man and one woman. In simplified terms, the marriage covenant involves a male and female coming together and pleasing God in their union. As a couple ascribes to please God, they are pleased also. When I use the term "please," I focus on the idea that as God's creatures, our goal should be to give Him the highest honor we can.

The contamination of the marriage model God created has come at the expense of being free moral agents.

What the Bible Says About Free Moral Agency[4]

Genesis 1:26

God tells us what He is doing at the beginning of the Book of Genesis. His project, His work, began with the formation of man as a physical being in the bodily form of God, and it will not end until humanity is in the nature and character image of God.

To accomplish this, God gave men free moral agency to enable us to choose and follow His way and assist in developing His image in us since we cannot be in His image unless we voluntarily choose to do so. Then, the character is

---

[4] Ritenbaugh, J. W. (1995). "The Covenants, Grace, and Law (Part Twenty)." from https://www.bibletools.org/index.cfm/fuseaction/Topical.show/RTD/cgg/ID/667/Free-Moral-Agency.htm.

genuinely ours and truly His because it is inscribed in us as a result of what we have believed and experienced.

God is not merely eternal. He is supreme in every quality of goodness; in Him, absolutely no evil dwells. In the Bible, this goodness is called holiness, which is transcendent purity. It permeates every aspect and attribute of God-like. God's character is holy and flows out from Him in acts of love, making it impossible for Him to do anything evil. This is the state towards which He is drawing us.

The law must be seen in this context. If we tear the law from the context of God's purpose, then we can come up with anything we want to say about the law. We can say, "Oh, it is all done away," or "We do not need to do this." However, we cannot tear it away from the purpose of God, and there is a reason for this.

Does God abide by the law? The creation screams at us that He does! Everything He creates operates by law, and it does so because it came from His wonderful, orderly, and organized mind. It reflects what His mind is like because this is how He is. He is a law-abiding God.

However, we cannot see Him - not literally, with our eyes. It is here that faith enters the picture: We can see evidence of Him, and we can believe what He says. His law outlines the way that He lives. It is the way of this holy, law-abiding God.

2. Accountability Element

I hate to be a discouragement to anyone. Still, every marriage and sex within marriage had to do with populating the world. Enjoying the intimate experience was secondary to filling the earth. So, God's original purpose for marriage was to fill the earth.

Sarah and Abraham's biblical account, where they agreed on Abraham having a child with Sarah's Egyptian handmaid Hagar, can be found in Genesis 16. What stress this decision had to develop between Sarah and Hagar significantly was when Sarah was made to feel inferior to Hagar. She fussed with her husband over the matter. Hagar hurried away from her mistress but returned and gave birth to Abraham's son Ishmael after angels visited her.

In Genesis 17, when Abraham was ninety-nine years of age, God proclaimed his name: "Abraham" - "A father of many nations" and provided him with the agreement of circumcision. Abraham was given the conviction that Sarah would have a child. Right away after that, Abraham and Sarah were visited by three men. One of the visitors told Abraham that Sarah would have a child upon his appearance one year from now. While at the tent entry, Sarah heard information exchanged, and she snickered to herself about the chance of having a kid at their age. Sarah, before long, became pregnant and bore a child to Abraham at the exact instant anticipated. Abraham, then, at that point, one hundred years of age, named the child "Isaac." Isaac would become pivotal in the scriptural account, fathering Jacob, the inevitable Patriarch of the Israelites.

Too often, marriage is approached as a time to enjoy the person you are married to only. Again, a couple must take seriously that they are married to the person of their choice until the end of their physical life. The commitment should be grounded in the fact that God put people together to propagate the human race. Somewhere, humanity has gotten its wires crossed on this crucial inflection. God made a part of His reasons for two people to come together in a lifetime commitment.

Policing or parenting your spouse are not accountability elements that flow well in your relationship. But you need to work hard at being accountable to one another. It allows for your marriage to develop a healthy oneness with your spouse. After all, this is the person you promised to be with "until death does you part."

When accountability is lacking, the natural boundaries in marriage are undoubtedly compromised. This leaves a crack in your marriage, allowing destructive interferences such as divorce or infidelity to creep into a promising relationship. Some areas should be placed on high alert and regularly discussed with the one you have committed to your future. These focus areas are finances, relationships, decisions, and technology. These conversations provide a level of mutual accountability in your marriage and should be visited with regularity.

Finances

Finances, simply put, mean money or assets. When you enter into a marriage covenant, you promise to share everything you presently own with the one you covenant your life with. That includes all bank accounts, 401k's, life investments, homes, cars, boats, farms, dogs, and cats. It would help if you shared these things and always be a topic of discussion. The absolute truth is that you have a love affair with your possessions. Before you married your spouse, you were married to your money and possessions! The Word of God says in Matthew 6:21 (KJV), *"For where your treasure is, there will your heart be also."* You must openly discuss your finances and treasures and regularly share your heart with your covenant partner.

Statistics have proven that money is one of the significant issues in relationships and the source of conflict in marriage. Prenuptial agreements society challenges marriages. This cultural mindset has proven to be damaging to the entire institution of marriage. It promotes a spirit of distrust among spouses by encouraging agreements that are not worth the paper it is written on, plus the idea that it is okay to hide and protect personal bank accounts. The married couple needs to see their finances and bank accounts as assets for each other. They need to be able to see their wealth and help the marriage as a whole. Make it a priority to discuss money with each other openly and regularly.

Accountability in your finances helps both spouses understand and agree upon the spending, budget, expenses, and debt. Discussing these things while using Godly wisdom undoubtedly guides you into a spirit of oneness. Set a monthly budget together. This allows for each of you to get and remain on equal footing. No one should be left in the dark and have to question or ask, "Where is the money at?" There will always be clear expectations: "Day in and day out." Eliminate undue stress and frustrations through consistent communication about your budget. This communication level eliminates overspending and prevents doubt and distrust from entering your covenant relationship.

Relationships

God feels a certain way about your marriage relationship! This is what He says in Genesis 2:24, *"Therefore shall a man leave his father and his mother, and shall cleave unto his wife: and they shall be one flesh."* Be open and accountable about the time you spend with friends and coworkers. You should spend the bulk of your time with your spouse! It is important to guard your heart against deep emotional connections with other folks, especially the opposite sex. Do the right thing and use the constraint to avoid situations that lead to temptation or present you as a person of wrongdoing.

Your spouse must know about your relationships outside of marriage. Some spouses feel they must have deep friendships outside of their marriage.

Still, it would help if you assured them of these platonic relationships, giving them free access and a level of comfortability with them as well.

As we reflect on Genesis chapter 2:24, we can see how important marriage is to God. He first implores the newly married couple to separate themselves from their familiar support system. In the Scripture, He says mama and daddy. Then, He instructs them in the next phase of their marriage covenant, which requires that they build a stronger and deeper relationship with one another. This relationship allows them to persevere through the challenges that await them in life.

Then He gives them a final step or rather promises they will have a successful marriage. He promises, *"And they shall become one flesh."* To a certain degree, this is the icing on the married cake. It is the glue that binds a marriage until death. Only God can take two individuals from different backgrounds, bring them together, and operate as one. Certainly, we find it difficult to understand God's strategic plan for marriage with our finite minds. The good news is that He does not require the married couple to understand every intricate detail but to obey and take advantage of what the detail has to offer. Again, the relationship with your spouse must remain your number one priority.

Decisions

Every decision you make, you are making it for one marriage. Because marriage is God's idea, your marriage entails three persons: you, your spouse, and the Holy Spirit. A husband and wife must work as teammates to advance their marriage. The Scripture reminds us of the one flesh portion of God's model: *"And they shall become one flesh."* The *"Become one flesh"* doesn't just happen. It requires commitment and being sold out to your spouse, just as a believer should be sold out to Christ. Absolute trust in anything and anybody demands work.

Great sports teams become great when they learn to trust and commit to one another. When Magic Johnson played with the Los Angeles Lakers from 1979 to 1991, he won five NBA championships. He led the league in assists during some of those seasons. Magic learned how to trust multiple players on the team. Because they trusted him, it influenced them to make significant decisions with the ball and position on the basketball court.

It would help married people if you acted as a united team, not as partners living in a house together. Choices, particularly significant ones that influence both of you, should be discussed together. Your mate can bring a great deal of substantial contribution to the marriage's overall success.

Marriage isn't ideal for finding that you have different perspectives on significant issues! Shared responsibility demonstrates the craving to counsel and include your life partner in everything essential to the relationship. Likewise, examining important choices before marriage concerning where you will live, youngsters, vocations, etc., will be helpful.

Technology

Without responsibility in the innovation zone, the entryway is open to permit vulnerabilities in your relationship. Having responsibility programming introduced on your telephones, tablets, and PCs creates a climate of straightforwardness for all gadget action.

Each spouse should make all their usernames, passwords, records, web-based life accounts, web history, and so on open to one another. In addition to the fact that this communicates trust with one another, it also serves to connect with pertinent information if anything should happen to your spouse.

You can access accounts and essential data in their temporary absence or death. Exemptions would apply with occupations requiring classification from the life partner in clinical, lawful, or directing fields.

Solid, adoring connections depend on great correspondence, trust, and straightforwardness. Shared responsibility in marriage gives a considerable advantage to empowering these characteristics in the relationship!

3. A God-Directed Marriage

I am not sure that everyone is seeking "A God-directed Marriage." Statistics prove that many marriages are generated from other interests than men and women agreeing in a marital relationship. In Psychology Today, the writer raises the question, "Is Love Essential to Marriage?"

In her book on the verifiable setting of marriage, Stephanie Coontz (2005) shows that this ideal became unavoidable just around two centuries earlier: "People have reliably become enchanted, and all through the ages, various couples have worshipped each other significantly. In any case, only now and again in history has love been considered the chief reason behind getting hitched." Coontz further argues, "In various social orders, love has been seen as an appealing aftereffect of marriage yet not as a substantial avocation for getting hitched regardless."[5]

Likewise, Pascal Bruckner (2013) fights that marriage was holy beforehand, and if it existed using any means, love was a kind of remuneration. Since reverence has become crucial in marriage, love is viewed as holy, and marriage is an assistant.[6]

Suitably, connections have declined while divorces, unmarried associates, and single-parent families grow. Bruckner observes that fondness has prevailed upon marriage. However, at this point, maybe pummeling it from within.

Considering fiery, wistful love as essential in marriage has overhauled marriage, zeroing in on it in our lives. It has also, regardless, made connections more temperamental and problematic. Whether or not to leave a marriage where love isn't vigorous is imperative for particular couples and wistful compromises become a primary concern.[7]

---

[5] Coontz, S. (2005). Marriage, a history: From obedience to intimacy or how love conquered marriage, New York: Viking.
[6] Bruckner, P. (2013). Has marriage for love failed?, Cambridge: Polity.

[7] Ellen, B. (2010). "Love in the Fourth Dimension " Annual Review of Psychology 61: 1-25.

Chapter 2:
Learn It, Live It

A marriage commitment requires spouses to commit to learning all and everything about one another. This is serious learning. The driving force to find out about your spouse is so that both spouses can equally build a relationship that garnishes the potential to last unto death as death becomes the separation factor. One must strongly desire to learn and draw closer to your spouse.

After all, when you met, perhaps you began as friends, but getting to know each other moved your relationship to become significant others. Then, a commitment in marriage beyond the infatuation for each other, you did not learn much about one another. Consider what you had to work through. Your spouse now, or spouse in the not-too-distant future, for the most part, has a background, and the way they were parented and raised is different from yours. For example, one of you may be the outgoing and the other the silent type. One of you was raised in a two-parent home, while the other was in a single-parent home. And even if you both were raised with the same number of parents, many variables still influence a couple's union and devotion to one another.

1. Pay Attention

Commit to learning details about your spouse. Details have always been the deciding factor in just about everything. For example, taking your car to get a $10 car wash is one thing. Having your car cleaned at a car salon, where the work is detailed, is another. In the $10 wash, you get the outside of the car washed and possibly vacuumed inside. When a vehicle is detailed, you also get a wash outside and a vacuum on the inside. Still, the detailer pays attention to cleaning adequately. The detailer works extra hard to remove all the outside and inside discrepancies. He goes an extra step and shampoos the carpet as well. He wipes down the seats, dashboard, and other car areas to make it look and feel new again. Finally, he sprays the car inside with an air freshener to smell a sweet aroma. Because you understand the difference between the two types of car washes, you are willing to pay three to five times more to get the details that help your car look and feel new again.

When you pay attention to your relationship's details, you can respond and make better decisions in ways you had not considered. You need to know your spouse's likes and dislikes. If their favorite color is red and their least favorite is yellow, you know when getting them gifts and what color schemes are off-limit. Do they enjoy holding hands, rubbing feet, hugging, and cuddling? How about enjoying late-night movies and early-morning breakfasts?

Do you know what makes your spouse happy and sad? What are their hot buttons? Do you know what to do to help calm them down? These questions should be of great concern to you concerning your spouse. Put another way, you should be willing to put in the extra effort and go above and beyond to understand your partner's needs and desires, big and small. Your relationship is a lifelong commitment, so it's crucial to be invested in it and ensure that you're doing everything possible to make it a success.

The details are the things that make your relationship special. These things make your commitment different from all other married people. Details continuously signal your spouse that you love and care about them. The details can beautifully present you even when you miss the mark.

2. Commit to Learning

When will you stop making excuses about your spouse's important things because you have not prioritized them? Just as one would commit to learning a specific discipline or craft, spouses need to engage in the same manner. Why is it important to commit to learning everything you can about your spouse? You are studying your spouse to commit more profoundly to your relationship. Even though commitment is a learned behavior, many relationships never experience the level of commitment God requires in the marriage model He created. For the most part, two people come into a marital relationship with little or no experience. When you get a new job, it does not matter if you are familiar with what you were hired to do; the company automatically puts you in training. They want to ensure that you learn the job's details. They understand the more you know, the more committed you are, and your value creates better production and output for the company. As a more highly trained employee, you place yourself in a better position for advancement. Many companies offer training modules that allow you to advance as your knowledge grows because it positively affects their bottom line.

Your marriage can benefit somewhat in the same manner. Think about it. Your spouse is like the employer, and you are like the employee. The company signed an agreement with you to be a part of their team. Which means they want to invest in you. The investment entails committing to learning as much as possible to be efficient for the company. As a lifelong partner, you must hunker down, learn, and embrace the details about your spouse. Your spouse is your MVP. Suppose you are going to "win" in your marriage. In that case, your spouse must be able to operate at their highest level as often as possible. To have a successful marriage, you must be aware of and work on the small things that matter to your spouse.

In other words, it's important to pay attention to your partner's needs and desires, even the small ones. This could involve things like remembering their favorite coffee order, making them a cup of tea when they're feeling sick, or giving them a massage after a long day. When you show your spouse that you care about the little things, it shows them that you love and appreciate them.

3. Refresh

You should always work overtime to hear and learn your spouse's heart in your marriage. Outside of God, the things your spouse has to say should be your main priority. Once you've learned how to listen and have committed to learning from your spouse, you must constantly push the refresh button to remind you of the things you have learned about your spouse. Every marriage is privileged to what I call a "refresh button." I consider this button to be more of a moment you may have as a spouse to recapture something previously learned in your marriage to improve it. Refreshing yourself daily with the details and nuances that matter the most with your partner for life can help keep your marriage healthy. Proverbs 10:7 reminds us, *"The memory of the just is blessed..."*

Because marriage is a journey, it is impossible to quickly grasp the total experience marriage has to offer. Spouses must find a way to learn what is essential to each other and commit to successfully navigating the journey together to bring God glory and enjoy the journey created by God. You are empowered to hit the "refresh button."

Chapter 3:

Sunup to Sundown

Marriage is a covenantal agreement. "Marriage does not rest within the criteria of a contract but rather that of a covenant. A fundamental difference between a contract and a covenant is that a contract is cut between two human parties and agreed upon as an honor. Legal proceedings are in place to enforce such private agreements. The marriage covenant is different because it is between a man, a woman, and God. Certainly, some people get married and do not believe in God. Yet, they follow the prescriptions traditionally associated with a covenant, not a contract. A covenant rests on the concept of a power higher than man, which gives proper authority to carry out any particular end the covenant seeks to attain."[8]

"It is the complete union of two people. When a couple is married, they are not simply "allies" or "friends;" they are joined together, and society is obliged to recognize that they are one.

For a marriage to be a complete union, those entering the union must engage in a total spiritual, emotional, legal, and physical collaboration. Marriage is not exclusive to a man and a woman because society is bigoted or hateful; the truth is that only a man in his distinctiveness and a woman in her distinctiveness can form a complete union.

Robert George of Princeton University has given an extensive legal and philosophical analysis of this question, specifically regarding marriage. He and his co-authors have done an outstanding job of articulating, from a legal and scientific standpoint, the fact that only a man and a woman can make this complete union.

---

[8] Osborne, S. (2012). "Marriage is not a Contract, it is a Covenant." from https://bearingdrift.com/2012/05/21/marriage-is-not-a-contract-it-is-a-covenant/.

The social engineers within the LGBT activist orbit demand that the government changes what constitutes a marriage that is attractive for homosexual couples to participate in. But the marriage covenant does not derive legitimacy from the government; if the Commonwealth of Virginia were to be dissolved tomorrow, no one's marriage would be any less legitimate. Because the government merely recognizes the marriage covenant for legal purposes, it still has no authority to change marriage parameters. The Commonwealth of Virginia recognizes both same-sex and opposite-sex marriages.

Those who understand marriage to be a covenant should prevent it from being redefined from a legal standpoint and address the other challenges that face the institution. Too many today view marriage as a contractual relationship with services rendered and services attained. There is much "me" and not a lot of "we." "The answer to changing society's sometimes degraded view of marriage is not ultimately political; it requires something much more fundamental, a changing of the human heart."[9]

1. Get Up in Your Commitment

"If I should die before I wake, I pray the Lord my soul to take." My verse to this old prayer is, "If my spouse doesn't awake, I willingly give my soul to God to take."

Suppose we understand that a marriage is a covenant and not an agreement. In that case, we know we must commit to our marriages daily. A genuine commitment requires everything you have related to a marriage commitment. Your covenant is based on your sacrificial giving to your spouse. Both people in the marriage must give everything they have. It's been said that "marriage is a 50/50 relationship." The reality is that marriage requires everything you have to offer, and you make a special effort to search for ways to give more. The efforts you make in your marriage should never be seen as a sacrifice to you but instead experienced as a sacrifice to your spouse. Working a forty-hour job weekly should not be the pinnacle of success you bring to your marriage, especially when you consider you have committed another person's life intertwined with yours. How do you quantify someone committing their

---

[9] Ibid.

whole being to you? The proper response must be to give them everything you can give in return.

You and your partner should be committed to one another for life. No marriage can enjoy and maintain a healthy relationship operating on a peek-a-boo level. You are all in one minute, and the next, you are out. You go to bed at night, satisfying your intimate needs to wake up in the morning, not wanting to remain faithful in your commitment. Your mind operates separately from your heart, and you find yourself in a cloud of doubt that has you chasing a dream but realizing it is one of your worst nightmares. You must commit to giving your marriage everything you've got!

2. Walk Out in Your Marriage

Your commitment to the marriage must go beyond lip service. Spouses must demonstrate their love, compassion, and commitment to each other daily. Many married people make promises to each other that they do not keep. As a spouse, there is a more significant commitment to keep your promises to each other and walk it out in an essential way to you both. You walk out in your marriage by aligning your priorities correctly. Your promises at the wedding ceremony are alive, active, and well. You keep "to have and to hold" dear to your heart no matter what.

Everyone knows that love is action! True love is demonstrated, not talked about. The power released through love can only be released when it is carried out. The love that exemplifies this type of power has to be greater than Philos and Eros. The love you have for your spouse should encompass both of these. However, it should closely relate to agape. I say "closely related" because it is rare for a marriage to experience authentic, agape love, as Jesus demonstrated on the cross. This type of love does not require one to give love in return. 1 Corinthians 13:4-7: *"Charity suffereth long, and is kind; charity envieth not; charity vaunteth not itself, is not puffed up. Doth not behave itself unseemly, seeketh not her own, is not easily provoked, thinketh no evil; Rejoiceth not in iniquity, but rejoiceth in the truth; Beareth all things, believeth all things, hopeth all things, endureth all things."* Humankind is inconsistent in loving on this level! C. S. Lewis gives us a brief but concise lesson on four types of love in the Bible in Greek that is worth our attention.

Storge

The first one is storge, called affection or familial love. This word isn't used in the Bible, but the concept exists. Storge is based on familiarity. People love their family regardless of whether they are people they would be drawn to otherwise; family members often have nothing in common except familiarity and blood.

Eros

The second is eros, which is romantic love. Eros isn't a word that appears in the Bible, though it plays a significant role in many Old Testament problems. Eros encompasses sexual and romantic love and is the root word of the English "erotic." Lovers are often completely preoccupied with one another, filled with eros.

Eros is often associated with sexual desire and lust. Still, it can also be good in a marriage relationship when accompanied by and bolstered with other kinds of love.

Philia

The third is philia, which is friendship love. This word is used in the Bible. As C. S. Lewis wrote in his book, The Four Loves, "To the Ancients, Friendship seemed the happiest and most fully human of all loves." Philia occurs from bonding over similar interests. Whereas lovers are preoccupied with each other, friends are preoccupied with the same things. Friends, of course, care about one another, but similar interests attract them to one another. "Philia" is the opposite of "phobia," meaning those experiencing philia are drawn to one another.

Philia is often overlooked in modern culture but is encouraged in the Bible. In Romans 12:10, Paul urges the believers to be devoted to one another in brotherly philia. Philia can be strongly associated with agape as well. In John 15:13, Jesus said there is no greater agape than laying down one's life for one's friends.

Agape

The fourth is agape, and it could be defined as charity. However, we often think of charity nowadays as giving away money or things, which doesn't encompass all of what agape is about. Agape love is unconcerned with the self and concerned with the greatest good. Agape isn't born just out of emotions, feelings, familiarity, or attraction but from the will and as a choice. Agape requires faithfulness, commitment, and sacrifice without expecting anything in return.

Agape love, in the Bible, is love that comes from God. God's love isn't sentimental; it's part of His character. God loves from an outpouring of who He is. As 1 John 4:8 states, "God is love [agapos]," meaning He is the source of agape love. His love is undeserved, gracious, and sacrificial. We are to love God and others with agape love. Agape is a choice, a deliberate striving for another's highest good, and is demonstrated through action.[10] God set the standard for agape love by sending Jesus to die for us while we were still sinners.

3. Lay Down and Start

Successfully guiding your marriage requires strategic planning and action. Sometimes, you need to stop and process your experiences. Taking the time to process your marital journey can be like laying down and having an out-of-body experience. Without getting too far over into the science world, an out-of-body experience is when a person experiences the world from a location outside their physical body.

Because God has fashioned your marriage to encompass every need you have in the earthly realm, you must take a break and view your marriage from every perspective familiar to humankind. When you lie down and rest, you can gain a fresh new perspective on things in this life. When you wake up and start fresh, your thoughts can be clear. Your understanding can be broader, and the patience needed for your marriage can be more readily available.

---

[10] Roat, A. (2019). "What Does Agape Love Really Mean in the Bible?". from https://www.christianity.com/wiki/christian-terms/what-does-agape-love-really-mean-in-the-bible.html.

Chapter 4:
I Can Do Five

Five used to be worth something. It used to be worth much more than it is today. You could buy quite a bit with five dollars in dollars and cents, such as putting gas in the automobile, going to the movies, getting two hamburger meals, and buying a special gift. That was back then. Five dollars can barely purchase a snack or your favorite ice cream in a cone.

Five is very significant. Considering its representation in the Bible, humankind was created to God's deliberate specifications of having five senses, five fingers, and toes on each hand and foot. Five also represents the number of God's grace. As we look further theologically, we discover five great mysteries. They are the Father, the Son, the Spirit, Creation, and Redemption. After the man was created, he slipped and failed. The earth fell into a curse and was subject to damnation. Because the planet went into such a depraved state, it needed to be redeemed; therefore, the number five is the number of God's grace. The number five may also speak of man's inability and weakness. When 'man' is weak, he does need God's Grace. Man's incapabilities keep him in a position where God's Grace is always required.

In the idea "I can do five," many failing marriages end by year five.

In my research, I discovered some vital and detailed stats about divorce. I felt this information is noteworthy for this writing. When reviewing the stats, consider how blessed you are to have a healthy and thriving marriage before and after five years of marital commitment.

These statistics were gathered and published on Wilkinson & Finkbeiner, LLP, a law firm dedicated to performing divorces. This is a statement taken from the site. "At Wilkinson & Finkbeiner, LLP, we understand that any disputes regarding family law have the potential to significantly impact the lives of you and your loved ones in profound ways. Our San Diego family law attorneys are committed to providing the service and support you need to resolve your family law matters with as little stress as possible."

Divorce Statistics: Over 115 Studies, Facts, And Rates For 2020[11]

If you spend enough time perusing the internet, you'll find no shortage of studies, statistics, or facts about divorce. There seems to be a study looking into almost every possible factor that might affect marriages and lead to divorce. These studies have yielded some fascinating and, in some cases, downright shocking information about divorce in the United States and the rest of the world. Just in case you don't have twenty hours to spare (it may or may not have taken this long to create this list), we have compiled a nearly exhaustive list with every divorce statistic, study, and fact that we could find. As we move through 2020, our San Diego divorce lawyer team has provided everything you need and possibly more about divorce.

COVID-19 Pandemic Divorce Statistics

As a result of the COVID-19 pandemic and varying states of lockdowns all over the United States and the World, we may be in for the most significant single-year increase in divorce in decades. We keep track of any reports and data that come out over the next year. We know so far: Jurisdictions worldwide and nearly every city in the U.S. have reported significant increases in domestic violence. Relationships experiencing problems are likely being stressed to breaking by factors such as the lockdown, financial strain, and political discord. We won't have a complete picture of the fallout until 2021 at the earliest in the U.S.

US Marriage and Divorce Rates Over Time

1. As of 2016, marriage and divorce rates in the U.S. are decreasing. Recent studies have shown that millennials choose to wait longer to get married and stay married longer, and are the primary driver of declining marriage and divorce rates in the U.S.

2. The marriage rate in the United States is currently 6.8 per one thousand total population.

---

[11] Wilkinson & Finkbeiner, L. (2020). "Divorce Statistics: Over 115 Studies, Facts, And Rates For 2020." from https://www.wf-lawyers.com/divorce-statistics-and-facts/.

3. The U.S.'s divorce rate is 3.2 per one thousand population (as of 2014, the latest year of data from the CDC. (with fort-four states and DC reporting) This is known as the "crude divorce rate." Although helpful in describing changes in divorce rates over time, the crude divorce rate does not provide accurate information on the percentage of first marriages that end in divorce. U.S. divorce rate per one thousand married women.

4. The divorce rate per one thousand married women is 16.9. Many experts feel this is a much more accurate measure of divorce than the crude rate.

5. The divorce rate per one thousand married women is nearly double that of 1960, down from the all-time high of 22.6 in the early 1980s.

6. Almost fifty percent of all marriages in the United States end in divorce or separation.

7. Researchers estimate that forty-one percent of all first marriages end in divorce.

8. Sixty percent of second marriages end in divorce.

9. Seventy-three percent of all third marriages end in divorce.

10. The United States has the 6th highest divorce rate in the world.

1. Somebody Needs to Make up That Bed

In the United States, ambiguity in the division of family duties between working couples regularly brings about continuous exchanges, disdain, and pressure. A 2007 Pew Research Poll indicated that sharing family tasks were among the three most elevated positioning issues related to a practical marriage—third was dependability and great sex. In this survey, sixty-two percent of grown-ups said sharing family errands is essential to marital achievement. No distinctions of assessment were detailed among people, between more established adults and more youthful grown-ups, or between married people and singles.

Couples without a system for household tasks can get very resentful quickly—a look at the results of an in-depth study of middle-class families.[12]

Many people thought, at some point, it was crucial to make a lifelong commitment to someone in marriage. However, many of those people still struggle with some simplicities in married life after many years of marriage. They have not figured out who should handle making the bed and performing basic housework. So, they often find themselves caught trying to make sense of petty disagreements that slash at the core of their commitment. These should be easy choices, but many find these decisions uncomfortable.

What's your perspective on the ideal division of labor and the proper distinction between male and female tasks and roles in marriage? Many spouses have had disagreements about their respective chores and responsibilities at home.

What's your viewpoint on the ideal division of work and the best possible differentiation among male and female assignments and parts in marriage? Many couples have had contradictions about separate errands and obligations at home.

When you began to look all starry-eyed, the idea of how to split the responsibility of family assignments likely wasn't on your radar. Since you're married, perhaps you find regular tasks always there. They show up day after day, week after week. The reality is that they are always there. Discovering a commonly accepted approach to dealing with this part of your marriage is imperative.

The culture has added pressure on the different tasks' spouses must perform in their marriages. So, allow me to keep it simple. We refer to the roles as "male" and "female" roles. However, should a spouse be responsible for washing dishes while her better half has used his expertise to ensure the

---

[12] Klein, W., et al. (2013). "The Difference Between a Happy Marriage and Miserable One: Chores." from https://www.theatlantic.com/sexes/archive/2013/03/the-difference-between-a-happy-marriage-and-miserable-one-chores/273615/.

plumbing works correctly? Couples who are believers may imagine that such male/female differentiation is scriptural instead of customary.

The Bible doesn't explicitly uphold that thought; for instance, many feel that ladies should cook and clean while men handle the budget and invest the funds.

It is not necessarily the case that there is no premise for recognizing male and female marriage functions. The scriptures state that: "[God] made them male and female" (Matthew 19:4; Genesis 1:27). The scriptures give some indication or idea of sexuality. They are usually seen in those areas of family life that are most directly connected with childbirth, child-care, and child-rearing issues. Nonetheless, couples will generally follow their folks' model regarding straightforward tasks. If you saw your daddy come home after a long day at work and pound his chest demanding his dinner, you will most likely ascribe to that example in your marriage. This can cause issues if implicit presumptions and false impressions are permitted to come forth out of resentment and contentions over sharing family obligations.

There is no "correct" answer for splitting the chores in the home through our eyes. Be that as it may, there are various rules to remember as you work to determine this issue reasonably and adjustably.

There is no way around good communication. First, hunker down and talk about this part of your marriage relationship. The mere fact that you see the value in discussing what needs to be done and agreeing to a particular task empowers you and your spouse and even decreases pressure and struggles. Try not to underestimate anything. Lay every one of your presumptions, desires, and individual inclinations out on the table. Approach the circumstance as equivalent accomplices and work out a game plan worthy of both of you. You'll be happy you did.

Think decidedly. Advise yourselves that this is not painful brain surgery. Whenever you decide to share the load, you'll probably find the rest of the process unfolding smoothly and naturally.

Think about the reward. The workload can be lighter and more pleasant when you put your hands together. This is particularly obvious when both spouses work outside the home. A functional framework leaves you with more opportunities for harmony and more recreation for singular exercises. Working together like this can take more time for both of you. This can be seen as a valued time for intimacy and other activities.

Focus on abilities, not gender. Instead of underlining "male" and "female" errands, discuss which tasks you appreciate or wouldn't have a problem doing. Is there anything in the list of chores that fits your skill level better? Is there anything where you draw the liner? Could you keep it simple, guys? Let these ordinary propensities control your decisions.

There must be exceptions to the rule. This should be given. Step up for your spouse and handle the responsibility when they cannot answer the call.

Where they are stressed, busy, or dealing with sickness, they will indeed step up for you.

Remain adaptable regardless of how excellent and equivalent things appear toward the beginning of your assignment; you may need to make changes along the way. Sooner or later, one spouse may get a job outside the home. There is always the possibility your spouse may become ill or injured and can no longer function in their agreed-upon role. Always ascribe to what is correct for your marriage. Remain flexible no matter what. Make the necessary adjustments so things progress well in the marriage.

It is okay to write it down. It is fundamental to create a list of what needs to be done. This process helps everyone remember their area of commitment. Make sure to incorporate a diagram that conveys the work division as far as "yours, mine, and ours."

As you experience a detailed process, attempt to see it as an opportunity for both to work together rather than operate in conflict. You want to be in the best possible position to meet the many challenges launched against your marriage. You can gain an advantage by striving to understand each other and meet each other's needs. This is a great reason to incorporate these principles and put them into practice.

2. Home Cooking

Your meals are sacred. Biblically, breaking bread has always been an effective process for dealing with problematic issues. An excellent physical meal has proven to be a trusted process to give and receive a spiritually impactful thought that feeds the heart, soul, and mind.

Married couples who eat together are likelier to report maximum happiness in their relationship.

Whereas 67% of those who ate together scored seven out of seven for relationship happiness on the happiness scale, only 58% of those who ate apart were similarly happy. Slightly counterintuitively, couples who were the least happy in their relationship—scoring one out of seven on the happiness scale—were just as likely to eat together as those who were pretty happy—scoring five or six out of seven.

Couples who eat together are 19% more likely to enjoy their meal.

Specifically, we found that 74% of couples who ate together enjoyed their meal a lot, compared to 62% of couples who ate separately. And 36% of those who enjoyed their meal the least ate together, compared to 69% of those who enjoyed their meal most.[13]

I grew up on good, delicious, simple home-cooked meals. My mother cooked meals that were fulfilling, easy, and plenteous. We ate foods like red beans, slow-cooked with ham hocks served on top of rice, and sometimes with greens and old-schooled cornbread. My siblings (four brothers and two sisters) always had more than enough to eat. Sundays after worship were our sit-down meal. We splurged on good traditional food such as gumbo, fried chicken, chicken in brown gravy, greens, cornbread, macaroni and cheese, fried pork chops, potato salad, green beans, apple pie, and pound cake. She would use these special gatherings to talk to us about family matters. We would deal with issues that concern us individually and collectively as a family. We reported on school and even things happening within the community and church. Often, we would leave the dinner table informed,

---

[13] Benson, H. (2019). "Are Couples Who Eat Together Happier Together?". from https://ifstudies.org/blog/are-couples-who-eat-together-happier-together#:~:text=Specifically%2C%20we%20found%20that%2074,who%20enjoyed%20their%20meal%20most.

equipped, and prepared to move forward with more confidence that life would be all right.

As valuable as Sunday get-togethers were for my family and me, they are equally valuable for marriage today. Home cooking is a great place to share things that concern you. As a matter of fact, your conversations become home-cooked conversations with added value for both spouses. A home-cooked discussion is the perfect gathering to deal with unresolved issues and dissolve conflicts once and for all.

3. We Are in It for the Long Haul

The phrase "in it for the long haul" is familiar today. It means a determination to continue with something until it is finished successfully. Unfortunately, humankind is guilty of not holding up to this promise. Many people are discouraged simply because someone has reneged on a promise.

The commitment you made during your marriage ceremony, remember "to have and to hold from this day forward, for better, for worse, for richer, for poorer, in sickness and in health, to love and to cherish, till death do us part, according to God's holy ordinance; and thereto I pledge thee my faith."[14]

Five years of marriage only need to be celebrated if the marriage celebrates the fifth anniversary. If you made it five years, eat a wonderful intimate dinner together and prepare your relationship for the lifelong ("unto death do us part") commitment. From day one of your commitment, you must be in it until one of you expires. If you entered your marriage with an expiration date in mind, the chance your marriage can survive is "slim to none."

Mark 10:9, *"What therefore God hath joined together, let not man put asunder."* Every married couple is instructed to stay married. Why? Because God says so! Humankind does not respect the Word of God. So, the divorce rate is still very high. Many divorces happen because people often say the vows for the wrong reason. Some say the vows because they look at their marriage strictly from a carnal perspective. They see two incomes coming

---

[14] Stewart, M. (2021). "Traditional Wedding Vows for Your Ceremony." from https://www.marthastewart.com/7888175/traditional-wedding-vows#:~:text=%22In%20the%20name%20of%20God,cherish%2C%20until%20parted%20by%20death.

together. They see more prominent and more houses being acquired. They see the great sex they can frequently have. So, from that vantage point, there is a feeling that if things do not favor them or go in the direction they envisioned, they could call it quits. He says what He joined together; no man cannot separate. Someone may say they will not allow anyone to interfere in their marriage to the point they create discourse between spouses.

Surprise! That *"let not man put asunder"* includes you as a spouse. You do not have the authority to end your marriage whenever you want. Remember, your marriage is a covenant between you, your spouse, and the Holy Spirit. Whom have you consulted about not allowing your marriage to reach its committed goal?

I know you can go to the courts and legally file for divorce. Many marriages end on Irreconcilable differences. There are occurrences where individuals feel like they can't continue their marriage due to encountering issues.

If you file for divorce under hostile circumstances, you do not need to agree with your spouse on the reasons for the separation.

This means that if your divorce is contentious and you cannot agree on why you are separating, you can still file for divorce. The court will decide the reasons for the separation based on the evidence presented.

However, it is important to note that filing for divorce under hostile circumstances can make the process more difficult and expensive. It is also important to remember that the court is primarily concerned with the best interests of any minor children involved in the divorce.

What separates hopeless contrasts is another approach to classify your separation as a no-issue separate. This implies that the reason for separation can't be accused of one mate, as in to blame separations where one life partner would charge misuse and infidelity.

Even if you blame each other for the separation, it will not affect the practical issues of the separation, such as the division of property, child care, and the divorce settlement. There are consistent exemptions for this, obviously![15]

---

[15] Schultz, C. S. (2020). "Irreconcilable Differences." from https://mensrightsdivorcelaw.com/blog/irreconcilable-differences/#:~:text=%E2%80%9CIrreconcilable%20differences%E2%80%9D%20technically%20means%20that,other%20issues%20in%20the%20marriage.

So, how do you stay in your marriage for the long haul? I believe you accomplish this by trusting the one who created the marriage. He can fix anything He made. If you are in a marriage struggle to this degree, your challenge will be to trust God to straighten it out. Your resolve is available in His Word!

Chapter 5:
Feeding a Hungry Marriage

This chapter allows me to share my thoughts on three questions that can add real value to your marriage and help it last. I will share those three questions later. In the meantime, allow me to share a few things about feeding a hungry marriage. Couples deal with too many activities that can distract them and disrupt quality time. With technology blazing new heights, hyper-busy is the new normal; you are recognized and heralded for being very busy. Marriages are suffering as they attempt to keep their marital connection and intimacy afloat and are often placed on the sacrificial altar. Marriage expert Michele Weiner-Davis (1992) argues that the most significant contributor to the breakdown in marriages today is the lack of time together.

Since husbands and wives are often pulled in different directions, the strength of their relationship and marital satisfaction often suffers. Research confirms that couples who experience a lack of time together report lower marital satisfaction Umberson, Williams, Powers, Liu, & Needham, 2005). In the National Survey of Marital Strengths, spending time together was identified as one of the top ten strengths for happily married couples; 71% of happy couples agreed with the statement, "We have a good balance of leisure time spent together and separately" (Olson, 1980, p. 3). Conversely, only 17% of unhappy couples felt that they spent a healthy dose of leisure time together (p. 3). In the same study, researchers identified the lack of time together as one of married couples' top ten stumbling blocks. Over 80% of husbands and wives who struggled in their marriage identified insufficient couple time as a significant problem (p. 5). Finally, in measuring couple connection and closeness, 97% of happy couples reported enjoying free time together (p. 17). Of couples who reported they were unhappy in their marriage, only 43% said they enjoyed spending time together (p. 17). If couples want to strengthen their marital bonds, spending time together is not optional! President Dieter F. Uchtdorf (2010) recently reminded us that when it comes to family relationships, "love is spelled t-i-m-e" (p. 22).

Most couples are not likely to admit that their marriage relationship ranks at the bottom of their priority list. If they were asked, most adults would contend that their marriages and families are the most important priorities in their lives (Stinnett, 1985). However, how much time couples spend with each other and their families may indicate their feelings about their true priorities. Our priorities are driven by (a) what is scheduled and (b) to whom we are accountable; hence, what screams the loudest will receive the most attention. Doctors Les and Leslie Parrott (2006) have stated, "Time is made whenever we decide what matters most. A top priority gets more time. If you decide that collecting stamps is the most important thing in your life, you will begin to schedule your day around it, spend your money on it, and talk about it. Because you prioritize it, you'll make decisions that create more time for it" (p. 65).[16]

A marriage is a live experience to be lived out until death comes along and finishes the commitment. Marriage is a living covenant. Anything alive must be fed. Think about it. An ant as small as it is must continue eating for survival. Grass has to receive the proper amount of nourishment to remain healthy and continue growing. No matter what it is, if it is alive, it must eat.

So, your marriage must continue to eat the proper diet to be healthy and not end prematurely.

Nothing threatens the security of a man's marriage more than the thought of another man competing for the attention and affection of his wife. Nothing is more painful, disrespecting, insulting, belittling, and degrading than that. However, the man has nothing to fear if he and his wife trust God to keep them.

Every marriage can flourish when the couple works together as a team. There is an old saying, "Teamwork makes the dream work." This is apparent when a man and his wife decide that winning in life together is more important than keeping score separately. Great marriages put in hard work to succeed.

---

[16] Ogletree, M. D. (2010). "Healing the Time-Starved Marriage." from https://rsc.byu.edu/divine-design/healing-time-starved-marriage#weiner.

They trust the one who instituted it. Many are watching you, especially your children.

You can count on your children watching you and forming lasting opinions as they learn the pillars of marriage: love, commitment, and trust. They are influenced based on what they see in you. What an incredible opportunity you provide them when they gaze at your marriage and gain hope and encouragement. This will make them look forward to a commitment to marriage one day.

There is somewhat of a misnomer in marriage life. Too often, married people will sometimes let themselves go after they have tied their significant other into a marriage covenant. They develop bad eating habits, have no workout regimen, and even skip good hygiene. Husbands: The reason why other women look attractive is that someone is taking good care of them. Anything getting proper care will always look, feel, and sound better.

As a husband who finds himself drooling over another woman, taking better care of your bride makes sense. Let her get her hair, nails, and feet pampered regularly. Take her to get massages, and set aside a budget to take her shopping. There is nothing wrong with admiring a beautiful woman. God made them that way. Plus, you will be lying by denying that she is beautiful. But it takes a true man to make a woman admirable and beautiful. When you do carnally, you are displaying her value to you.

When a husband puts his wife above everyone and everything except God, it gives his wife the sense of security, stability, and honor she hungers for. Your marriage does not require a big house, an expensive car, or a million dollars to succeed. You can achieve all this while still enduring a miserable marriage. A successful marriage requires having the Spirit of God and His unselfish love at the core, honesty, and an undying commitment to each other.

Your honest commitment will have you praying for your spouse regularly in the morning, afternoon, and evening. The last thing you want to do is wait until there is a problem. Why wait until there is an affair, a revealed devastating secret, or a crippling disease? It would help if you didn't wait until something terrible happened. Please don't wait for the temptation to avail itself. Cover your spouse with prayer and blanket your marriage with the quilt of protective prayer.

Be careful with the people you choose to have hanging around. They can have a significant influence on your marriage. Friends can build or break your marriage; make your selection wisely. Perhaps you don't truly value your marriage; as you said, don't. You need to beware of marital advice from these folk hanging around you, especially if they are single people. No matter how sincere their advice may be, they are not married, so most of their advice will be theoretical and not from living real-life experiences. When you need Godly advice, you can get it from God-fearing, impartial, and prayerful mature couples. They have been tested by time and shaped by many trials.

The challenges marriages face are many. Never take your spouse for granted. The enemy will have you take advantage of your spouse's kindness and good deeds.

Respect them because your spouse proves to be loyal; they are not desperate. Don't misuse or abuse your spouse's trust. Trust is imperative to a marriage relationship. You can regret losing someone you committed your life to until death do you part.

Finally, the power of the tongue can be devastating to your marriage. That tongue, according to James 3:8, says, "But the tongue can no man tame; it is an unruly evil, full of deadly poison." It can reduce your marriage to ruins or raise it to very high peaks. At all costs, you cannot allow Satan to use your tongue to kill your spouse's image, self-confidence, and aspirations. Instead, let God use your tongue to build your marriage and bless and praise your spouse.

Here are the three questions I promised to discuss in this chapter.

1. What makes a marriage hungry?
2. How do you feed a hungry marriage?
3. Why feed your marriage?

1. Appetizer

"After a decade of marriage, birthing four mini-me's, and turning into a SAHM, I am beyond hungry. I am starving, actually. My appetite has become insatiable, and my cravings unsurmountable. Yet, it isn't food that I need to satisfy these hunger pangs. Not in the least.

I am hungry for passion, intimacy, and emotional stimulation. I desire the sex life of my wildest fantasies to come true and then some. I want to reawaken the woman inside of me. The one I laid to rest in order to transform into the selfless caregiver I must be to meet the demands of my roles as a mother and a wife."[17]

Kristina Hammer, aka The Aggravated Mom, is a Coca-Cola-guzzling, go-with-the-flow SAHM of four on her way to insanity and beyond. A writer by nature, blogger by nurture, and a poet at heart, she spills her heart onto the screen. She has been featured on sites like Scary Mommy, The Good Men Project, and Mama pedia. You can follow her personal blog at The Aggravated Mom or her column, To Insanity and Beyond, over at Sammiches and Psych Meds for more of her writing, and you can follow her on Facebook and Twitter so you don't miss out on the daily crazy in between.

What makes a marriage hungry? This question can be approached from several directions. Successful marriages require certain things to remain healthy.

2. Main course

How do you feed a hungry marriage? The main course of a marriage is the relationship between the two spouses. It is the foundation on which the marriage is built and the source of its strength. The main course of a marriage comprises many different ingredients, including communication, love, respect, trust, and commitment.

Here are some of the key ingredients in the main course of a marriage:

- Communication: Communication is essential for any healthy relationship but is especially important in a marriage. Spouses need to communicate openly and honestly with each other about their thoughts, feelings, and needs.

---

[17] Hammer, K. (2019). "Hungry for More Than This Adventureless Marriage." from https://realitymoms.rocks/adventureless-marriage/.

- Love: Love is the foundation of any marriage. It is the bond that holds the two spouses together and helps them weather life's challenges. Love is expressed in many ways, including words, actions, and touch.
- Respect: Respect is essential for any healthy relationship. Spouses need to respect each other's opinions, feelings, and boundaries. Respect also means valuing each other's contributions to the marriage.
- Trust: Trust is another essential ingredient in a healthy marriage. Spouses need to trust each other to be honest and faithful. Trust also means feeling safe and supported by each other.
- Commitment: Commitment is the glue that holds a marriage together. It is the willingness to work through challenges and to stay together for the long haul. Commitment is also about putting the needs of the marriage before your own needs.

The main course is delicious and satisfying when these key ingredients are present in a marriage. The spouses are happy and fulfilled in their relationship and can face life's challenges together.

In addition to the key ingredients listed above, many other things can contribute to a healthy and happy marriage. These things can vary from couple to couple, but some common examples include:

- Shared values and interests
- A strong support system
- A sense of humor
- A willingness to forgive
- A commitment to personal growth

If you are looking for a recipe for a successful marriage, there is no one-size-fits-all answer. However, focusing on the key ingredients listed above can create a delicious and satisfying marriage.

3. Desert

Why feed your marriage?

"Hostile contrasts" imply that an individual and their mate can't coexist enough to keep the marriage alive. This absence of getting along can cause an entire cluster of different issues in the marriage. It doesn't make a difference in what caused a fracture inside the marriage because of hostile contrasts.

Wellsprings of Marriage Problems

Connections offer the executives significant advantages for prosperity, life fulfillment, and stress; however, none are without difficulties.

These issues can strain a couple, yet working through them can either fortify their bond or push them apart, contingent upon how they handle their difficulties.

Soundly working through marriage issues can be troublesome, mainly because stressors in a marriage can emerge from various sources.

Cash Problems

The pressure of battling about cash comprises one of the most frequently referred to marriage issues.

As a rule, when couples participate in clashes about cash, their contest is genuinely symbolic of something else—influence battles, various qualities, needs, or different issues that encompass money.

Be that as it may, in intense monetary occasions, monetary pressure can cause more broad stress, more clashes over things irrelevant to cash, and money-focused contentions.

For instance, when one accomplice is amazingly worried over cash, they might not be so patient but rather more focused and significant; they may provoke the other accomplice about random things without acknowledging it!

Issues with Children

The approach of kids brings another likely wellspring of marriage issues. Youngsters are brilliant and can bring tremendous and significant blessings into our lives.

Nonetheless, having kids can bring extra pressure into marriage because children's caretaking requires more significant duties just as an adjustment in jobs, gives more feed to contradiction and strain, and decreases the measure of time accessible to bond as a team. This blend can test even the most grounded of relationships.

Day-by-Day Stress

Everyday stressors don't have to approach marriage issues, yet they can compound existing problems. When one accomplice has had an unpleasant day, they might be bound to be anxious when they return home. They may deal with struggle less expertly and may have less passionate energy to give to supporting their accomplice and their relationship.

At the point when the two accomplices have had a troublesome day, this is just exacerbated.

Similarly, as with monetary pressure, general day-by-day pressure can test tolerance and confidence, leaving couples with less to provide for each other inwardly.

Occupied Schedules

Marriage issues can result from excessively bustling timetables for a couple of reasons:

Couples occupied are frequently focused, mainly if they're not dealing with a lack of rest and things that will have them stressed.

Occupied couples may feel less associated because they have fewer ideal opportunities to spend together and more separateness in their lives.

Couples may not cooperate as a group (regardless of whether their duties are isolated on the off chance that they don't arrange to cover all obligations well). They may battle who's dealing with which family unit and social duties.

While occupied timetables don't prompt marriage issues, they introduce a test that should require special attention.

Helpless Communication

Maybe the greatest indicator of marriage issues is helpless correspondence or negative correspondence that misrepresents harming mentalities and elements inside the relationship.

Negative correspondence is so harmful. The scientist John Gottman and his group have had the option to anticipate which lovebird couples would later separate in light of viewing how they would communicate with one another for a short period.

Substantial openness is paramount; undesirable correspondence can prompt significant marriage issues.

Negative Behavior Patterns

Then, couples experience marriage issues that could be tackled if they could see their propensities and change them. Individuals don't generally settle on a conscious choice to contend over little things. They sometimes annoy one another and leave things in a mess for others to clean up.

Individuals get into pessimistic examples of relating, fall into sluggish individual propensities, or get into a groove they sustain without much forethought.

Luckily, these marriage issues can be chipped away. Any change can acquire a move in the relationship's dynamic, bringing positive outcomes, whether just one person moving forward to a viable difference in the relationship.[18]

---

[18] Scott, E. (2020). "Sources of Marriage Problems." from https://www.verywellmind.com/common-marriage-problems-and-solutions-3144958.

Chapter 6:
Say So

1. A Husband's Position in His Marriage Is the Leader!

The role of the husband in the Bible starts with leadership. The Bible explains that a husband should be a leader of his home and have healthy control of his life. 1 Timothy 3, speaking of two church leadership positions traditionally filled by men, teaches that an Overseer and Deacon must manage their family well. Verse 5 says, "For if a man knows not how to rule his own house, how shall he take care of the church of God?"

Gaining greater understanding, Ephesians 5:21-24 says, *"Submitting yourselves one to another in the fear of God. Wives, submit yourselves unto your own husbands, as unto the Lord. For the husband is the head of the wife, even as Christ is the head of the church: and he is the savior of the body. Therefore, as the church is subject unto Christ, so let the wives be to their own husbands in everything."*

Again, in 1 Corinthians 11:3, Scripture says, "But I want you to realize that the head of every man is Christ, and the head of the woman is man, and the head of Christ is God."

One of the essential functions of a husband in the Bible is to lead. Authority implies influence. A scripturally-based husband should impact his family positively. Husbands are not tyrants; they ought not to demand; they should not rule over their wives. All things being equal, husbands should impact their wives and families as per scriptural instructions. They ought to represent their voice and actions ascribed that carry greatness to God and incentive to their companion and family. A scripturally-based husband produces solid fruit and helps his wife thrive in every way.

Two concrete ways a husband influences his home are through provision and protection.

The function of the Husband in the Bible – Provider and Protector

The part of the spouse in the Bible begins with administration yet includes arrangement and assurance. A husband will never influence his wife if he does not care for her. He can demand, and she may follow as a result. Still, he will never truly have her heart unless he provides for her needs, cares for her well-being, and protects her physically and spiritually. As Scripture says: *"But if any provide not for his own, and especially for those of his own house, he hath denied the faith, and is worse than an infidel."* (1 Timothy 5:8).

"Husbands, love your wives, and be not bitter against them" (Colossians 3:19).

"Likewise, ye husbands, dwell with them according to knowledge, giving honour unto the wife, as unto the weaker vessel, and as being heirs together of the grace of life; that your prayers be not hindered." (1 Peter 3:7).

God loves His daughters and the children they bear. When He gives one of His daughters to a man, He wants the man to think about her. Scripture does not teach or endorse women and children being considered second-rate or inferior to men. Instead, He finds them so precious that He asks for special care to be given them, care that only biblically-based men can provide. Women are very capable of taking care of themselves. However, God did make men and women different. Thus, due to the physical nature and strength God gave men, He has charged them with providing and protecting their families.

The actual nature and strength are to be managed with grace and gentleness. God didn't make men reign over ladies, nor did He make ladies look out for men. He made them both supplement each other through sound companionship.

The function of the Husband in the Bible – Companion

The husband's function in the Bible is satisfied through the core of friendship. Ephesians 5:25-33 says, "^{25} Husbands, love your wives, even as Christ also loved the church, and gave himself for it; ^{26} That he might sanctify and cleanse it with the washing of water by the word, ^{27} That he might present it to himself a glorious church, not having spot, or wrinkle, or any such thing; but that it should be holy and without blemish. ²⁸ So ought men to love their wives as their own bodies. He that loveth his wife loveth himself. ²⁹ For no man ever yet hated his own flesh; but nourisheth and cherisheth it, even as the Lord the church:

³⁰ For we are members of his body, of his flesh, and of his bones. ³¹ For this cause shall a man leave his father and mother, and shall be joined unto his wife, and they two shall be one flesh. ³² This is a great mystery: but I speak concerning Christ and the church. ³³ Nevertheless let every one of you in particular so love his wife even as himself; and the wife see that she reverence her husband."

The connection between a husband and a wife is intended to be love, respect, and support. They are to help one another. This thought is presented toward the beginning of the Bible when God made Eve. Adam desired a companion, a reasonable helper, yet one couldn't be found until God created Eve.

Genesis 2:20-24 says, *"...Adam gave names to all cattle, and to the fowl of the air, and to every beast of the field; but for Adam there was not found an help meet for him. ²¹ And the Lord God caused a deep sleep to fall upon Adam, and he slept: and he took one of his ribs, and closed up the flesh instead thereof; ²² And the rib, which the Lord God had taken from man, made he a woman, and brought her unto the man. ²³ And Adam said, This is now bone of my bones and flesh of my flesh: she shall be called Woman, because she was taken out of Man. ²⁴ Therefore shall a man leave his father and his mother, and shall cleave unto his wife: and they shall be one flesh."*

This additionally prompts another comprehension of friendship. God made people with normal, physical, and passionate differences. Generally, where one is weak, the other is energetic and strong. A husband and wife can help each other by meeting the other person's needs through physical and emotional intimacy. 1 Corinthians 7:2-5 addresses this: "But since sexual immorality is occurring, each man should have sexual relations with his wife and each woman with her husband. The husband should fulfill his marital duty to his wife and the wife to her husband. The wife does not have authority over her own body but yields it to her husband.

In the same way, the husband does not have authority over his own body but yields it to his wife. Do not deprive each other except perhaps by mutual consent and for a time so that you may devote yourselves to prayer. Then come together again so Satan will not tempt you because of your lack of self-control." When our spouse's needs are adequately met through healthy companionship, the two can help each other live a successful life.

In conclusion, a couple cooperates as a team to create and grow a family through friendship. God arranged that each home operates under the specific roles of both a husband and a wife and that through this, they raise healthy children who honor God with their lives. Ephesians 6:1-3 says, "Children, obey your parents in the Lord, for this is right. 'Honor your father and mother' —which is the first commandment with a promise— 'so that it may go well with you and that you may enjoy long life on the earth.'" Children are blessed through the honor of their mom and dad working as one to prepare them in the way they should.

The husband's influence directs the companionship between a man and a woman through his provision and protection. It is covered by his caring, gentle, and graceful love for his wife and family. Without the scriptural roles being satisfied by a committed godly man, the nuclear family faces the challenges welcomed by transgression and worldly enticements. Satan wants to demolish the family, yet through Christ and good comprehension of the scriptures, the family is ideal for growing in God.[19]

2. A Wife's Position in the Marriage
Role of the Wife in the Bible - God's Plan for the Wife

The role of the wife is clearly described in the Bible. Although males and females are equal in relationship to Christ, the Bible gives specific functions to both the husband and the wife in marriage.

As wives, we are given these roles, among others:

Mentors - Titus 2:4-5 says, "Then they can train the younger women to love their husbands and children, to be self-controlled and pure, to be busy at home, to be kind, and to be subject to their husbands so that no one will malign the word of God."

---

[19] AllAboutGOD (2013). "Role of Husband in the Bible." from https://www.allaboutgod.com/role-of-husband-in-the-bible.htm.

Witnesses - 1 Peter 3:1 says, "Wives, in the same way, be submissive to your husbands so that, if any of them do not believe the word, they may be won over without words by the behavior of their wives."

Examples - 1 Timothy 3:11 says, "In the same way, their wives are to be women worthy of respect, not malicious talkers but temperate and trustworthy in everything."

Role of the Wife in the Bible – The Design Order of the Family Unit

When studying the role of the wife in the Bible, it is important to understand how God designed the family unit. There are ranks described—Christ, the husband, the wife, and then the children. You would not expect to walk into a doctor's office and be greeted by the doctor, measured and weighed by the receptionist, and treated by the nurse. Right? There are specific orders to things because that's what works. It's the same way with God's design in the family unit. It works smoothly when done His way.

God designed the husband as the leader of the home (1 Corinthians 11:3; Ephesians 5:23). The Bible describes this leadership as loving—not dictatorial, condescending, or patronizing of his wife or children. A husband's leadership is compared to Jesus' love for the church. This love is one of mercy, forgiveness, compassion, and selflessness. "Husbands, love your wives, just as Christ loved the church and gave Himself up for her to make her holy, cleansing her by the washing with water through the word" (Ephesians 5:25-26).

Ephesians 5 also speaks of the wife's role in the marriage. Ephesians 5:22-24 says, "Wives, submit to your husbands as to the Lord. For the husband is the head of the wife as Christ is the head of the church, His body, of which He is the Savior. As the church submits to Christ, wives should also submit to their husbands in everything."

Colossians 3:18-19 reiterates this concept. It says, "Wives, submit to your husbands, as is fitting in the Lord. Husbands, love your wives, and do not be harsh with them." These verses show that love and respect characterize the roles of both husbands and wives. If these are present, authority, headship, love, and submission will be no problem for either spouse.

Beth, a wife, explains it this way,

"The role we have as wives is encouraging and helping our husbands. We run into trouble when we try to make it any more or less. My mom used to teach a young married couple's class, and I will never forget her most 'valuable nugget' of truth. She always told them that the husband is the head of the home, and the wife is the neck. The neck supports the head and helps the head fulfill its duties."

Role of the Wife in the Bible – The Wife of Noble Character

Proverbs 31 also speaks of the role of the wife in the Bible. We learn of her worth to her husband and family, how she cares for those who need her, how she provides for her family, protects them, and shares her strength with others. She fulfills her responsibilities with grace and power. We also learn that a wife is a blessing to her husband. She is worth more than rubies! Wives can follow her example by living in the wisdom of God.

"A wife of noble character who can find? She is worth far more than rubies. Her husband has full confidence in her and lacks nothing of value. She brings him good, not harm, all the days of her life. She selects wool and flax and works with eager hands. She is like a merchant ship, bringing her food from afar. She gets up while it is still dark; she provides food for her family and portions for her servant girls. She considers a field and buys it; out of her earnings, she plants a vineyard. She sets about her work vigorously; her arms are strong for her tasks. She sees that her trading is profitable, and her lamp does not go out at night. In her hand, she holds the distaff and grasps the spindle with her fingers. She opens her arms to the poor and extends her hands to the needy. When it snows, she has no fear for her household, for all of them are clothed in scarlet. She makes coverings for her bed; she is clothed in fine linen and purple. Her husband is respected at the city gate, where he takes his seat among the elders of the land. She makes linen garments, sells them, and supplies the merchants with sashes. She is clothed with strength and dignity; she can laugh at the coming days. She speaks with wisdom, and faithful instruction is on her tongue. She watches over the affairs of her household and does not eat the bread of idleness. Her children arise and call her blessed; her husband also praises her: 'Many women do noble things, but you surpass them all.' Charm is deceptive, and beauty is fleeting, but a woman who fears the Lord is to be praised. Give her the reward she has earned, and let her works bring her praise at the city gate" (Proverbs 31:10-31).

3. The Creator's Position

The Holy Spirit in Your Marriage

Do you ever call on the power of the Holy Spirit to be at the center of your marriage? Married couples forget to call on this help for their marriage. We encounter problems at work, raising our children, finances, and many daily issues. Most of us have attended a marriage seminar or read an article and told ourselves we will work toward the perfect marriage. The next thing we know, we find ourselves in a debate that ended without a win-win result. Don't condemn yourself because all is not hopeless. Learning marriage principles is excellent, but we need the power of the Holy Spirit if we want long-term change. Malachi 2 says that marriage is God's "Holy Institute." Anything "Holy" is a target for the enemy.

Here is a personal testimony.[20]
Married Fifty-One Years to Richard Salazar 1968-83. Employed for the City of Los Angeles.
Educated: Pasadena City College and Berean Bible College
Co-Founder New Harvest Christian School
Missionary: Five years in England
New Harvest Christian Fellowship - Administrator
http://www.newharvestnorwalk.com/
F.O.C.I.S. non-profit - Board Member:
One day, I was studying on my bed. My husband was exercising in our garage and was coming up the steps. As he was coming up the steps, I turned my head, and in a flash, I saw a demon crouched down in my bedroom, ready to attack my husband. Now, I don't believe Christians can be demon-possessed, and my husband is a very Godly man. Good marriages are his primary target. I shared this story in my marriage class. I thought all the women would walk out and think I was crazy. After my class was over, one wife came up to me

---

[20] Salazar, N. (2011). "The Holy Spirit in Your Marriage." from
https://loveyourspouse.org/2011/10/19/the-holy-spirit-in-your-marriage/.

with tears in her eyes. This may sound funny, but she told me that she was so glad to hear that. She said she felt like her marriage was constantly attacked and thought she was the only one. To hear that a demon had the nerve to come into my bedroom made her feel she was not alone in battling for a good marriage.

On our own, we cannot consistently pursue a great marriage.

2Cor.13:14 "The grace of the Lord Jesus Christ, and the Love of God, and the communion of the Holy Spirit be with you all."

You need the communion of the Holy Spirit in your marriage.

Jesus was giving His disciples a new leader:

John 14:26: "But the Helper, the Holy Spirit, whom the Father will send in My name, He will teach you all things, and bring to your remembrance all things that I said to you."

John 16:13: "When He, the Spirit of truth, has come, He will guide you into all truth; for He will not speak on His own authority, but whatever He hears, He will speak; and He will tell you things to come."

The minute you accept Christ as your Savior, the Holy Spirit comes into your life.

God loves the Holy Spirit so much that He chastised the children of Israel for their disobedience.

"But they rebelled and grieved His Holy Spirit; so, He turned Himself against them as an enemy." (Isa.63:10)

David knew that the secret of his greatness was not him but the power of the Holy Spirit.

"Do not cast me away from Your presence, and do not take your Holy Spirit from me." (Psa.52:11)

Let the leading of the Holy Spirit replace your natural reactions.

"For if you live according to the flesh, you will die…" (Rom.8:13-14)

The Holy Spirit produces fellowship with God and an effective relationship with our spouses.

This is how the Holy Spirit impacts your marriage:

- He empowers you to fight sin (Gal.5:15-16)
- Helps to produce the fruit of the spirit in you (Gal.5:22-23)
- Daily directs your life (Rom.8:14)
- Assist your marriage to glorify Jesus (John 16:14)
- Convicts you of sin (John 16:18)
- It gives them the power to be Christ-like (Eph.3:16)

Ask the Holy Spirit right now to help your marriage succeed.
The Holy Spirit will teach you not to quench His Spirit.
He will teach you how to keep your marriage fresh and vibrant!
You have tried everything else; give Him a try.

Chapter 7:
The Telling Three T's

Ephesians 4:32: *"And be ye kind one to another, tenderhearted, forgiving one another, even as God for Christ's sake hath forgiven you."*

Every marriage has emotional and physical needs. You must be guilty of surging up your spouse's emotional needs by telling them how much you love them and reinforcing their place and value in the marriage relationship. Marriages are starving because spouses tend not to understand the importance of supporting their spouses emotionally. For example, it is very important to support your spouse when something catastrophic has happened. If they lose a loved one, you should aid their emotional health more than anyone else.

1. Tripping

The word 'tripping' used in this form is slang for not loving your spouse. Your marriage can be hungry for sanity. This is the area where spouses have complete control. You decide how well you treat your spouse. Bad treatment, in this sense, can be considered a negative power.

How often have you found yourself detached because you did not agree about something? These can be challenging moments for many reasons. One reason is that the enemy can use your disconnection to eat at the fabric of your commitment. He has the ability to chip away at the covenantal agreement you made with God at the consummation period of your marriage. He can have you tripping with your spouse!

Tripping in that every question asked receives an ungodly response in foul words, tone, and spirit. The enemy would like nothing better than to create bad blood between you and the one to whom you have dedicated your life.

2. Treatment

The Harry and Meghan Story by Marie Jackson BBC News

In the summer of 2016, the two were brought together on a blind date by a mutual friend in London.

"Beautiful" Meghan "just tripped and fell into my life," Harry later told the press, and he knew immediately she was "the one."

After just two dates, the new couple went on holiday together to Botswana, camping out under the stars.

They fell in love "so incredibly quickly," proof the "stars were aligned," said Harry.

To the British press, their romance was catnip. Here was a golden couple who could draw vast crowds, speak the language of younger generations, and sprinkle royal stardust on any cause.

The wedding of Prince Harry and Meghan Markle was held on May 19, 2018, in St George's Chapel at Windsor Castle in the United Kingdom. Prince Harry's groom is a member of the British royal family; the bride, Meghan Markle, is American and previously worked as an actress. But from the time of their marriage, she was treated like royalty by those she served and the rest of the world.[21]

Treat means to behave towards someone or deal with something in a particular way. The question to you is, how are you treating your spouse? The answer should be without hesitation; you treat them like kings and queens.

Typically, both the king and queen are treated with the utmost respect. When they make a request, they expect it to be carried out quickly and correctly. Inadequate treatment is a lot like cheating. It can have you holding back the sweetness you have preserved for your life partner. Your spouse deserves your royal treatment and vice versa. Husband, your wife is committed to you.

---

[21] Jackson, M. (2020). "The Harry and Meghan story." from https://www.bbc.com/news/uk-51049276.

Regardless of any conflict you may have, a wife should remain committed to her husband.[22]

"Vehicles require regular maintenance for optimal performance, just like relationships demand time and effort to sustain a deep connection."

3. Trusting

Trusting Equals Fruitfulness

Trust—*First published Mon Feb 20, 2006; substantive revision Mon Aug 10, 2020*

Trust is important, but it is also dangerous. It is essential because it allows us to depend on others—for love, advice, help with our plumbing, etc., especially when we know that no outside force compels them to give us these things. But trust also involves the risk that people we trust will not pull through for us. We would not need to trust them if there were some guarantees that they would pull through. Trust is, therefore, dangerous. We risk, while trusting, the loss of valuable things that we entrust to others, including our self-respect, which can be shattered by the betrayal of our trust.

Because trust is risky, it is particularly important when warranted. In this context, "warranted" means justified or well-grounded. The trust is rational (e.g., based on sound evidence) or successfully targets a trustworthy person. If trust is warranted in these senses, its danger is minimized with justified trust or eliminated altogether as with well-grounded trust. Leaving the risk of trust aside, one could also ask whether the trust is warranted in being plausible. Trust may not be justified in a particular situation because it is simply not plausible; the conditions necessary for it do not exist, as is the case when people feel only antagonism toward one another. This entry on trust is framed as a response to the general question of when trust is warranted, where "warranted" is broadly construed to include "justified," "well-grounded," and "plausible."

---

[22] Lancer, D. (2019). "Toxic Relationships." from https://www.psychologytoday.com/us/blog/toxic-relationships/201904/signs-serious-relationship-problems.

The Nature of Trust and Trustworthiness

Trust is an attitude we have towards people we hope will be trustworthy. In contrast, trustworthiness is a property, not a philosophy. Trust and trustworthiness are distinct, although, ideally, those we trust will be trustworthy, and those responsible will be trusted. For trust to be plausible in a relationship, the parties must have attitudes toward one another that permit trust. Moreover, for trust to be well-grounded, both parties must be trustworthy. (Note that here and throughout—unless specified otherwise—"trustworthiness" is understood in a narrow sense according to which X is trustworthy for me just in case I can trust X.)

Trusting requires that we can (1) be vulnerable to others—vulnerable to betrayal in particular; (2) rely on others to be competent to do what we wish to trust them to do; and (3) rely on them to be willing to do it.[2] Notice that the second two conditions refer to a connection between trust and reliance. Trust is a kind of reliance for most philosophers but not *mere* reliance (Goldberg 2020). Instead, trust involves dependence "plus some extra factor" (Hawley 2014: 5). Controversy surrounds this extra factor, which generally concerns why the trustor (i.e., the one trusting) would rely on the trustee to be willing to do what they are trusted to do.

Trustworthiness is likewise a kind of reliability, although it's unclear what type. Clear conditions for trustworthiness are that the trustworthy person is competent and willing to do what they are trusted to do. Yet this person may also have to be ready for specific reasons or have a particular motive for acting (e.g., they care about the trustor).[23]

---

[23] McLeod, C. (2020). Trust, Stanford Encyclopedia of Philosophy.

Chapter 8:
Where Are We Now?

1. No More Disagreements

There must be a commitment between spouses to "no more disagreements" because of a lack of understanding. If you have been married for a while, you probably say the guy has lost his last mind. The reality is this. As long as you remain in your marriage covenant, you will never agree on everything one hundred percent. Disagreeing can be a healthy exchange in your marriage. When you learn how deep your love is for one another, caring and compassion begin to surface during periods of disagreement and reconciliation.

No more disagreements mean that as a couple desiring to live out a marriage that will give God glory, you will do all you can to operate in harmony with your spouse. You will consider your spouse's point of view and search for an immediate resolution. You want peace, and you understand the value of operating as one.

Many marriages struggle because they do not understand one another clearly.

Here are some warning signs that your relationship may be in trouble. It doesn't necessarily mean your relationship is at the quitting stage. But it does reveal that it is in trouble and needs serious attention. However, it is salvageable, and the love connection can be restored. It is at a place where you both need to have honest communication and may need professional help. Here are some things that may be plaguing your marriage. Many marriage counselors would refer to these as typical characteristics of codependent relationships and suggest they may be the underlying issue in marriages struggling to gain their footing.

1. Inflexibility or repeated unwillingness to compromise on decisions like social activities, chores, moving, and having children.

2. Putting your feelings and needs ahead of your partner's, without showing care or providing support for their feelings and needs, can be described as a lack of consideration for your partner.

3. Meddling by parents.

4. Repeated deference to a friend or relative over your partner's objection.

5. Repeated instances of critical, undermining, blaming, sarcastic, disrespectful, or manipulative comments. This is verbal abuse.

6. A pattern of withholding communication, affection, or sex. This is often a sign of veiled anger.

7. Arguments or problems that don't get resolved.

8. Raging or name-calling.

9. Keeping secrets.

10. Passive-aggressive or aggressive behavior, including shoving or breaking objects.

11. Controlling behavior, including giving unwanted advice, ordering, or withholding money for affordable expenses to control.

12. A secret romantic relationship or pattern of flirting.

13. Use of drugs or alcohol that impacts the relationship or work.

14. Too much time apart if it causes your partner dissatisfaction.

15. Persistent resentments, judgments, or disappointments.

16. There is generally a lack of open communication or communication that lacks personal content. This may not be a problem for some couples with low intimacy needs. Their relationship functions well like a business partnership.

17. Breakdown of trust. This can be caused by numerous things, such as dishonesty, using personal information against your partner, unreliability, broken promises or agreements, violating personal boundaries, or infidelity.

18. You need constant attention, validation, or reassurance – whatever's given is never fulfilling for very long.

19. Some subjects are off-limits or you're afraid to talk about.

20. Violating personal boundaries, such as disrespecting your request not to be called at work, not having confidential information repeated to others, not being criticized about something, or not reading your mail.

It is essential not to score your marriage or spouse but to raise issues you may need to address and talk openly and honestly about when reviewing this list. Many relationship problems can be resolved if you and your spouse commit to healthy, assertive communication. This communication level requires both spouses to be open, direct, respectful, honest, and personal. This is when you can put everything on the table to bring your relationship back closer together.

If you overthink the process, your situation will probably worsen because you are afraid, to be honest. Why would you fear being unthinkably honest with the one person you have committed your life to? Perhaps because you are struggling to see your spouse and best friend in the world, you can only see the truth as something that will upset them and seriously jeopardize your promises to each other. Part of your challenge has to do with possible hurt and pain associated with being honest and transparent in any situation. This depth of commitment often disarms your defense, protecting you from hurt and the critical blame game. You learn to communicate and problem-solve with others in the family growing up. Unfortunately, if the examples you linked from were not good, there lies the problem facing you in your marriage today! You never learned how to be assertive, so struggling to communicate with your spouse on a very high level can be extremely challenging. However, when your relationship is challenged, you hunker down and do what you must to make up for love. This is the same love that brought you through the friendship stage into a committed marriage designed to take you to the very end.

Allow me to share a thought about the longevity of marriage. I believe the Bible teaches in regards to the lasting nature of marriage. We see three main passages relevant to the discussion: Matthew 19:1-12, Matthew 22:23-33, and Romans 7:1-3. The Bible teaches that a man and woman are bound in marriage until death. Upon death, the marriage is no longer binding. Paul, writing to those called "saints," true believers in Christ, whom God's grace has redeemed through their faith, is not given the law of eternal marriage.

There is no textual evidence that this has been changed, as some claim in the Bible.

An imbalance of power creates other relationship problems. One partner attempt to dominate the other through aggression, control, or emotional or verbal abuse. This is damaging to the relationship and the self-esteem of the other partner. It's not uncommon in relationships with an addict or narcissist. One partner can control the other through neediness, demanding attention or validation, or playing the victim, expecting the other person to make them happy.

Repetitive negative relationship patterns stem from problems originating in childhood, such as disrespectful communication, lack of nurturing or accessible emotional expression, a controlling parent, violation of boundaries, neglect, witnessing parental conflict, mental illness, addiction, or abuse. A variety of dysfunctional parenting styles cause shame and undermine a child's self-esteem, which continues into adulthood.

Shame and low self-esteem thwart love, intimacy, and assertive communication. Individuals with shame and low self-esteem don't feel worthy of love or respect and withdraw emotionally or push their partner away directly or indirectly. They abuse or allow abuse, imagine being criticized when they're not, and are so afraid of losing the relationship that they smother or control their partner, withhold negative feelings, and build resentment.

The struggle for intimacy requires the courage to face unhealthy behavior and attitudes and be vulnerable. It entails overcoming defenses of denial, withdrawal, control, or placating to avoid a real connection. Don't ignore or argue about these problems, deepening the division between you and your partner.

Instead, go to couples counseling. Because relationships are dynamic systems, when one partner behaves in the manner listed above, it damages the relationship. Similarly, studies show that the relationship improves if you improve your self-esteem and communication skills. One spouse in individual therapy often makes positive changes, and the marriage changes for the better.[24]

2. Who Is Living in This House?

Do you wonder if you know the person you are married to even though you have been committed to them for many years now? Have you discovered that the things that appear to bring joy and happiness in your relationship are not as effective now? Can you detect a need to understand your spouse's needs better?

Many married couples' marriages began shaky because they were trying to make sense of learning to live with each other and discovered the many challenges they are confronted with and must overcome to have the marriage they had hoped for. Take a peek at the marriage situation, even if you started your relationship from a platonic friendship. I believe friendships are platonic by definition; would you agree?

A platonic friendship is a relationship between two people who could, in theory, feel some type of way toward each other.

When one considers a marriage, it is a friendship on steroids. Your platonic friendship involves some of your emotions. Still, all feelings are involved when you enter a marital commitment. That means new feelings will be introduced into the relationship that was not there before. You concealed them, which was your way of protecting them. The problem is that your spouse is not prepared to handle your new feelings about this or that. This will put a strain on your relationship.

Even though you were unprepared to deal with new emotions that suddenly appeared in your relationship, you must confront them somewhat head-on. Because you truly love your spouse, you begin to consider how you will deal with the unexpected and minister to your spouse's needs. You must devise a resolve to handle this avalanche of emotional refuge that does not give you space to properly pick through it and come away with a desirable solution.

---

[24] Lancer, D. (2019). "Toxic Relationships." from https://www.psychologytoday.com/us/blog/toxic-relationships/201904/signs-serious-relationship-problems.

As quiet as it is kept, this subsequential emotional roller coaster can run aground quicker than you can say, "Save me, Lord!" as Peter was able to do when he began to sink after he attempted to walk on water. (Matthew 14:22-33 NLT)

3. A New Car

How many people enjoy that new car-buying experience? The answer is not many. Buying a vehicle has always been an expensive process and intense stress. But if you ask the same people how much they enjoy that new car smell that comes with a new car, the response will be totally different!

A new car and a new marriage are both exciting new beginnings. They both require a lot of investment, both financially and emotionally. And they both have the potential to bring a lot of joy and happiness into your life.

However, some key differences exist between a new car and a new marriage.

A new car is a physical object. It can be seen, touched, and driven. A new marriage, on the other hand, is an abstract concept. It is a relationship between two people.

A new car is also a relatively short-term investment. Most cars last for 10-15 years. A new marriage, on the other hand, is a long-term investment. Most marriages are designed to last a lifetime.

Finally, a new car is something that can be replaced. If your new car breaks down, you can buy a new one. If your new marriage breaks down, replacing it is much more difficult.

Chapter 9:
Marriage On Automatic

When we consider something operating automatically, we immediately visualize that thing running independently. In other words, it has no operator to control its functions.

When I was a young teenager, I aspired to drive an automobile. When I became a young adult and could drive legally, I was prepared to drive a manual-operating vehicle or an automatic one. I could drive either one because my brother Edward Leroy showed me how to operate cars equipped with manual or automatic transmissions. He was a drag racer and mastered the manual shifting process tailored to the weekend drag racer. Shifting manually will allow the driver to build up the RPMs and get more speed in a shorter time, pushing the vehicle to go very fast.

Even though the cars I owned primarily were all automatic transmission operated when I was much younger. However, I was always fascinated and wanted to drive a manual vehicle just for its thrill. As I matured, I lost interest in driving manual cars. I like cars that shift automatically. I was no longer interested in dealing with the fuss created by shifting a vehicle from first through fifth gear. My focus changed. I wanted to get in the car, start it up, put it in gear, and drive to my destination. Marriage can be seen somewhat like that. When one first gets married, one tends to have an exploratory mindset. One wants to see the world and the axles it spins on. But then, that marriage began to mature and no longer seek life's great thrills. This marriage has survived the storms and the rages that have come against it from its inception. This marriage has arrived at a place where it doesn't need extras to function correctly. It no longer receives marriage counseling but gives counseling. This marriage is strong and has learned the art of squashing issues and eliminating problems before they take hold.

1. Driving with One Hand on the Wheel

It would be good for every new driver to adhere to a strict training process. Driving a vehicle is simple. However, it is very challenging to carry out the requirements in order to be a safe driver. Mainly, one must focus and remain on that level until one arrives safely at the destination. This seems to be very difficult for young drivers. Many seem not to understand the depth of the responsibility behind driving an automobile. So, they falter in taking it seriously, leading to not following proper fundamentals while operating a vehicle. They teach the new driver to place both hands on the steering wheel in driving school. This will give the driver proper control of the vehicle while driving. Because of immaturity, many young drivers will take risks and drive with one hand. They want to show off while they're behind the wheel.

2. Distractions Without Disruptions

Every distraction does not have to be a disruption. Many things in life can distract you. However, we must work hard to prevent them from arresting our full attention. Take driving down the highway. For example, you will see things that temporarily distract you. There is trash flying across your windshield, people hanging out of the window, blasting sirens blaring from emergency vehicles, and many more possible distractions. However, it would be best if you did not allow whatever gets your attention to disrupt your focus on navigating safely on the highway. Otherwise, letting distractions disrupt you and take away your control can lead to a horrendous end.

One dictionary says that a distraction is a thing that prevents someone from giving full attention to something else. As it relates to our discussion, something else is marriage. Younger couples tend to be more distracted in their relationships than more mature couples. They are distracted by many issues, such as money, communication, trust, and other people, to name a few. However, they must learn not to allow distractions to disrupt the marriage. Marriage couples must take their commitment to one another extremely seriously. When they say, "Until death does us part," they must mean it beyond the crowd gathered to witness their union in becoming one. The vow ceremony happens in one day. The newly married couple's vows are designed to last for a lifetime.

Disruption is a disturbance or problem that interrupts the flow of one's marriage. They then affect the marital process. Disruptions can bring a seemingly healthy marriage to its knees and a bitter end.

This is a culture of disposable things. No matter how deep we get into the disposal mindset, some things should last a lifetime. The Bible is clear on its position even though during Jesus' day, the Jewish community did not see marriage as a common belief that would last a lifetime. Jesus taught His disciples in (Matthew 19:9 ESV) "I say to you: whoever divorces his wife, except for sexual immorality, and marries another, commits adultery." This is one of the things that the disciples found most surprising about their Master. Jesus stated His view on the matter succinctly:

Look at the reaction of the disciples in Matthew 19:10 (ESV):

"The disciples said to Him, "If such is the case of a man with his wife, it is better not to marry."

The disciples were not used to hearing conversations like this about marriage based on the text! Again, divorce was common among the Romans and the Jews during Jesus' earthly ministry. There was a Roman Jewish historian, Josephus, also a divorced man. In some of his writings, he believed that a man was permitted to divorce his wife "for any reason whatsoever."

I think many Christians view marriage's permanence differently from previous cultures. The lesson Jesus taught His disciples is that marriage should last forever. He indicates an exception that had to do with sexual immorality. This could be a catch-all phrase to deal with sexual behavior outside marriage.

When a marriage ends in a divorce, it is not because true love wasn't involved or ran its course. Often, it is because it experienced a distraction that led it to be disrupted. Extramarital affairs, simply put, are disruptions. The romance didn't just happen. It started as a distraction. Someone outside of the marriage got the attention of your spouse. In other words, your spouse was distracted. If the man was distracted in the relationship, it had to do with what he heard or saw physically in the person that distracted him. The same goes for the woman in the marriage. When one allows themselves to be distracted to that degree, it will often lead to a marriage that has been destroyed.

3. Spouse Forever

The word of God teaches in John 15:13 (ESV)

"Greater love has no one than this, that someone lay down His life for His friends." The Bible goes on and says in Proverbs 18:24, "But there is a friend who sticks closer than a brother." These verses talk about the sustainable unconditional love that Jesus has for humanity. This love is known as agape. I believe the love that loves without any conditions is the type of love God designed for those who would commit themselves to a marriage covenant. This type of covenant requires or demands unconditional love. Consider this: some of the best marriages began as friendships. This is where two people vowed to be friends with one another forever. Unfortunately, many married couples never connect the dots. Sometimes, they view their friendship as a casual relationship that can end at a moment's notice.

Who is your BFF? I grabbed this definition from a site called socialbuddy.com on the web. It said BFF stands for Best Friends Forever. In simple words, this represents two people who are each other's best friends, with a bond shared between these two people that will last a lifetime. This phase can also describe a close friendship characterized by permanence and trust. 'Best friends forever' points to a marriage relationship without the frills. Outside of your relationship with Christ, it is the most critical relationship two people could ever commit themselves to be lifelong partners.

"Best friend" is what a marriage is constantly working to become. Every marriage relationship that is committed to standing the test of time should be working at having a solid and undying bond. The goal should be to close any disparity gaps, block physical and spiritual interference between friends, and agree to maintain an unmeasurable amount of wholesomeness between the two.

One can draw different conclusions about what the term "forever" means. I agree with God's word, and the songwriter Jonathan Nelson says, "Forever is a long time." Forever has to do with one's lifespan. Some newborn babies don't even live for a few minutes after birth. In contrast, others grow into adulthood way beyond the average lifespan. The reality is that at some point, physical life ends. So, their forever-related life ended for the baby, who didn't live very long after birth.

To my dearest spouse, I can't believe it's been these many years since we said "I do." It feels like we were standing at the altar just yesterday, promising to love each other forever. And yet, in that time, we've shared so much together: joy, sorrow, laughter, tears, and everything in between.

Through it all, our love has only grown stronger. You are my best friend, my lover, and my soulmate. I can't imagine my life without you.

I promise to love you unconditionally, to support you through thick and thin, and to always be there for you.

I can't wait to see what the following years and beyond hold for us. I know we can face any challenge together if we have each other.

I love you more than words can say.

Let's finish this thing,

Spouse Forever

Chapter 10:
The Display

Displays make prominent exhibitions of things whereby they can be easily seen. So, they are designed to be seen. Displays often convey a specific message to a specified audience in advertising and marketing. Much of the creativity used in this process is motivated by statistical data and information. In other words, the displayed message usually is well thought out and planned. In this chapter, I would like to share the idea that the display related to marriage should be considered valuable and well thought out.

Claude Monet said this about complementary colors in 1888: "Color makes its impact from contrasts rather than from its inherent qualities. The primary colors seem more brilliant when contrasted with their complementary colors."

Claude Monet's Complementary Color Scheme

Complementary colors are directly on opposite sides of the color wheel. So blue is a complement of orange, red is a complement of green, and yellow is a complement of violet. Complementary colors provide striking visual effects when paired together.[25]

Comparing a marriage to a color wheel is a creative and insightful way to think about the different aspects of this complex relationship.

I don't know if the great artist Claude Monet or even Rembrandt, for that matter, ever considered their color theory could be seen in a marriage relationship. However, here are some of how a marriage is like a color wheel:

---

[25] Scott, D. (2017). "How The Impressionists Used Complementary Colors To Great Effect." from https://drawpaintacademy.com/best-colored-pencils/.

Primary colors

The primary colors of the color wheel are red, yellow, and blue. These colors cannot be created by mixing other colors. In a marriage, the primary colors could be seen as the three essential ingredients: love, respect, and trust. Without these three things, building a solid and lasting marriage is difficult.

Secondary colors

The secondary colors of the color wheel are green, orange, and purple. These colors are created by mixing two primary colors together. In a marriage, the secondary colors could be seen as the different aspects of the relationship created by the primary colors. For example, love and respect create intimacy and connection. Love and trust create safety and security. Respect and trust generate loyalty and commitment.

Tertiary colors

The tertiary colors of the color wheel are yellow-green, yellow-orange, red-orange, red-purple, blue-purple, and blue-green. These colors are created by mixing a primary color with a secondary color. In a marriage, the tertiary colors could be seen as how primary and secondary colors interact. For example, love and intimacy can create joy and passion. Love and security can create contentment and peace. Respect and loyalty can develop a sense of belonging and family.

Balance and harmony

Just as a color wheel is most harmonious when the colors are balanced, marriage is most successful when the different aspects of the relationship are also balanced. This means there should be a balance of love, respect, trust, intimacy, security, loyalty, commitment, joy, passion, contentment, peace, belonging, and family.

Change and evolution

Just as the colors on a color wheel can change and evolve, so can a marriage. As the spouses grow and change, the relationship will also grow and change. This is a natural process, and it is important to be flexible and adaptable to maintain a solid and healthy marriage.

Overall, comparing marriage to a color wheel is a helpful way to understand the different aspects of this complex relationship. It is also a reminder that a successful marriage requires balance, harmony, and flexibility.

What is the difference between a man and a woman? Science is chiming in on the creation of man. Let me suggest that you cannot take any of it to heart.

First, God made man and woman unique, uniquely different. Everything God made, He made it good. Hebrews 2:7, "Thou madest him a little lower than the angels; thou crowned him with glory and honor, and didst set him over the works of thy hands." Psalm 139:14 KJV ". . . for I am fearfully and wonderfully made." Suppose you do not know who you are. In that case, you find it challenging to understand what God was doing when He established a man and woman in a marriage covenant. For many, marriage is a daunting quest—a journey with no clear path and a fight with no clear winner.

However, marriage is as simple for many as 1, 2, 3. Some marriages have accepted the biblical model. Also, today, some marriages pattern themselves after biblical examples. These marriages can be misleading. They are nestled with many issues between the man and the woman that ultimately show themselves throughout the life of the marriage. They are operating as God intended them to work. The man understands his role, and the woman understands her role. Together, they can operate a marriage that is pleasing to God. Because of the biblical record recorded in Genesis chapter 2, every marriage has an opportunity to be successful. Unfortunately, many marriages will never experience what God intended for them because they will not take the time to learn what God has said about the model He created for marriage.

"Will a man leave his mother and father and cleave to his wife, and they shall become one flesh." We can detect the plan and God's marriage process by looking at what the Scripture suggests about marriage. *"Will a man leave . . .,"* is the first challenge God offers to a man entering into this new relationship. Man will quickly respond, no! His response has reverberated down through the ages. He feels he does not need to work on God's plan according to God's instructions. Man, always thinks that his way will be better than God's way. More specifically, the married couple is fully responsible for their marriage from the beginning. He must be willing to take his family to a place where God can begin to weed them together for them to become one

flesh. So, here is the deal. Man must be willing to link up with a person he doesn't know and separate from his mother and father, people he has known his entire life. These people were there when he was born and catered to all of his needs from infancy to adulthood. He must have the courage to put his whole trust and faith in instructions given by an invisible God to allow him to do what he would consider impossible. "The things which are impossible with men are possible with God." (Luke 18:27)

(Proverbs 20:12)

"The hearing ear, and the seeing eye, the Lord hath made even both of them."

There are a lot of marriages that do not take into serious consideration that many couples are watching them. I believe every marriage has an audience. Sometimes, the audience can be neighbors, close friends, strangers passing by, and anyone taking the time to observe a couple.

Because marriage is on display, every married couple should realize several things. Many people are looking at your relationship. So, your marriages will be seen on purpose, caught unaware, and every couple should be willing to change their view.

1. Seen on Purpose

Some couples are convincing in how they present themselves as a happy couple. They often go overboard to portray an image that does not truly represent their relationships. You can find them arguing constantly but not in the presence of anyone outside their home. They have mastered perpetrating and disguising themselves from others. Many of them don't like one another. However, they agree to put up with one another in the best interest of children, Family, and material accumulation. They bought into the image of marriage and have become satisfied with modeling it. They are unaware of the power experienced by touching and agreeing with one another. They tend to focus primarily on their disagreements and have come to terms with the idea that they may never make lasting changes to enhance their relationship. Married couples that have settled for this perspective in their marriage have certainly thrown in the towel. Truly, they no longer want to be married. At best, they go out in public together to project a closeness that is not in the relationship. At this stage, a marital relationship suggests something went wrong after the

"I do" ceremony. As a married couple, certainly, you have memories of your wedding ceremony. You can remember the period coming up to your wedding day. Some can recall the butterflies and jittery they felt in their bodies. Perhaps your ceremony was laced with primping and dipsy doodles, and how can you forget the pomp and circumstance?

Perhaps you spare no expense. Couples getting married have shelled out anywhere from $50-$50,000 in their "I do" ceremony. Part of that was that they wanted those watching to be convinced they were committed to the person they were marrying. This was the grand announcement! The idea was to project physically what one was feeling mentally, physically, and emotionally.

Every marriage can struggle at this stage because they have been influenced by every example of marriage they have ever seen. Some of those examples were poor. Poor standards can trainwreck an honest beginning. Children grow up and get married, and their models of marriage will come from mom and dad. If mommy and daddy cussed and fussed with each other, they would adopt cussing and fussing in their new marriage as they struggle to work through disagreements. Let me remind you that they had VIP seats in their parents' marriage relationship. Even when their parents tried throwing them a curve ball as if their seats were in the nosebleed section, the young couple soon realized they were close enough to remember every detail.

2. Being Seen Unaware

How many know that people can see you whether you realize it or not? I called that, being seen unaware. First, they can see you because they're watching you. Everyone is looking for an example for whatever it is they are doing. They don't necessarily request an example, but you can trust they are looking for models. In other words, many couples always look at other married couples to see how they relate. Other people are noting the jesters and conversations they feel they can identify with. It has been said that we learn better by example. I remember my college days; a visual presentation was consistently more effective than a lecture.

People are searching for answers to the marriage equation. The top six search engines are Google, Bing, Baidu, Yahoo!, Ask.com, and DuckDuckGo.

However, it's estimated Google processes approximately 63,000 search queries every second, translating to 5.6 billion searches per day and around 2 trillion global searches per year. The average person conducts between three and four searches each day.[26]

When you are unaware, you're being seen, you are subject to doing things you wouldn't normally do. In other words, your behavior may not be stellar. A security camera can bear witness to this position. We live in an age where cameras are everywhere. People are equipped with high-power cameras at their fingertips. At the same time, you can now find security cameras everywhere you turn. Security cameras play a pivotal role in nabbing criminals in many criminal investigations. For example, suppose the criminal broke into a store. In that case, the camera will display how they were able to do that and give valuable investigative information in helping prosecute the criminal.

I am not indicating that you are a criminal couple. Or a couple that commits crimes, for that matter. However, I am making you aware that many eyes are watching you when you're unaware. That's an excellent thought, considering your marriage is 100% on point. Reality check! None of us are operating at 100. We all need to continue putting in valuable work to improve our relationships with our spouses, not for our benefit only but for those we know are watching. Those we are unaware of are gazing at our behaviors from their observation platforms. Couples should want to influence others through the examples they demonstrate positively.

3. Change the View

In most cases, when you see something, you do not like, you can do something about it. Yes, you do not have to fix your eyes or heart on anything you find undesirable. You can change the view.

Let's be honest: marriage is a journey through life. It is a very serious commitment to someone you feel comfortable taking your life journey. Sometimes, it can be compared to walking the red carpet with bright lights

---

[26] Lenhart, A. and M. Duggan (2014). "Couples, the Internet, and Social Media." from https://www.pewresearch.org/internet/2014/02/11/couples-the-internet-and-social-media/.

and flashing cameras on the marriage journey. One of the main differences is that eyes can be all over you, and you do not know it. Many are watching you as an example, and you are watching other marriages as you try to understand better what marriage is all about.

"To be fully seen by somebody, then, and be loved anyhow—this is a human offering that can border on miraculous." —**Elizabeth Gilbert.**

All of this, watching and observing others is like collecting and storing data. But just like in the digital environment where space is a premium, you must decide what data you will keep and what information you will discard. Bad examples of marriage should be discarded without reservations. We all love our kinfolk. However, they don't always do the right things, which means they can project poor examples of marriage. It is easy to adopt the models you see in them because they are your family, and you are around them regularly. So when their marriages head in the wrong direction, you must be careful to strive for the marriage covenant's legitimacy when you make vows to your spouse and the Holy Spirit at your wedding ceremony.

Sometimes, you must change your view of marriage to maintain a good view. Have you ever looked through the lens of a microscope? The image is often blurry and hard to identify when you first put your eye over the lens to see what is beneath. But as you begin to make adjustments to the telescope, the picture starts to focus. This will allow you to view the image in greater detail better. You can then collect the necessary data to understand that image better. Sometimes, you must cancel out some of the many examples you've seen. This will allow you to search for better models to follow. Regarding marriage, you need to learn what was right in that marriage you observed and what was wrong.

Sometimes, a couple must push past the not-so-good marriage examples for their relationship to grow. Sometimes, the only way to do that is by changing their view. In other words, blot out the bad examples. This will open your relationship up to new opportunities.

Chapter 11:
Gaining While Maintaining

Race car drivers are the perfect examples of gaining while maintaining. They can operate at a consistent speed with the understanding of positioning themselves to win the race.

This idea is relatable regarding marriage moving and growing towards tremendous success. No marriage can be successful if it does not find its comfort zone and maintain it. Like the race car driver setting out to win a race, marriages must find their own pace. From the start of marriage until year five, marriage often moves at a blissful pace. However, the pace or relationship created in that marriage will begin to go through a developmental process beyond that point. This occurs because the more a spouse learns about one another's needs, it will affect everything in the relationship. Every couple can use a few things to position themselves within their relationships, leading to valuable stability in their marriage. Your marriage must perform intentional acts of kindness, work on Marriage development, and have a tighter connection.

1. Intentional Acts of Kindness

It is most important that the spouses are intentional about what they do for one another. This idea has to do with the intentionality that is a must in a successful marriage relationship desiring to please God. When entering a marriage covenant with another person, each individual should commit and say, "I intend to be this type of person to my spouse." After the agreement has been entered into, both spouses should remember the covenantal commitment and constantly work to carry out the pledge.

A great value develops in the marriage when spouses are intentional. You must show your spouse kindness. What is the meaning of kindness? It means doing nice things without expecting good things in return; kindness is more than just being nice. Do you want people to describe you as "nice" or "kind?" There can be a lack of sincerity in being just nice. Not only when it's easy to be kind but also when it's difficult. Kindness is a state of mind. Has someone ever done something nice to you, and all you want to do after that is pay them back? If we all focus on kindness, we create a state of mind for change. It's more extensive; it is a movement that can be triggered by a person acting on a purpose. Kindness is love; love is kind. Think about what love entails and what it means to love someone. When we offer these behaviors to others, we make people feel good, transmit hope, promote peace, and show the power of kindness. Kindness is grace. We are human, and therefore we make mistakes. If we could all remember that none of us are perfect, we would be kinder to each other and offer the same grace.

Kindness in a marriage requires you to be intentional with your spouse. You want every act of kindness expressed to your spouse to come from your heart. Again, kindness is a grace. Grace is a God quality made available to every person made in the image of God.

"You can accomplish by kindness what you cannot by force." – **Publius Syrus.**

2. Marriage Development

Since marriage is between two different people in many ways, it has to be developed. I believe great marital relationships come from two people who engage themselves through quality and honest platonic friendship. No marriage comes ready-made. A spouse has to learn the little nuances about their spouse that will help the positive development of their relationship.

Amos 3:3: "How can two walk together unless they are agreed?" In a marriage, you have to learn how to agree. This is why it is crucial to know the details about your spouse. Each spouse should take time out and discover who the other person is with whom they made a covenant. Do you know your spouse's favorite color? How about their favorite food? Have you discovered the things that get under their skin? What is their passion? What makes them happy? What makes them sad? Do you care about what they care about? How much time do you spend learning more about your spouse? Finally, did you know that there are new things to discover about your spouse as your marriage matures in age? Priorities change and shift as your marriage gets older. If you said I do at age twenty-five, be prepared for things to change as you age. Of course, the "I do" should not change. Many reading this book probably can identify with acting a certain way earlier in their marriage than where they are right now. Many things you did as a married couple at the beginning of your marriage have changed. You no longer hang out all night or randomly spend money as you once did. You desire to be home at a specific time and budget more. These are changes you felt necessary for your relationship to continue to grow.

As your relationship continues to grow and move forward, you will need to make changes as you learn what your spouse will need. This is an excellent way to empower them to be all they can be in the relationship. It would help if you always searched for ways to support your efforts and energy, allowing your marriage to develop as it moves forward.

3. A Tighter Connection

You may have a glorious marriage, but there will always be room for improvement. It is imperative that you remember why you fell in love with your spouse. This will always help them to experience your affection. This is when you can rely on your "love language" to see you through.

When times get tough, you must move quickly to forgive and make haste to accept forgiveness. It is unrealistic to expect your spouse to meet every need you have. When you're left feeling let down or frustrated, remember that only Jesus can understand you completely because His Father made you in His image and likeness. At that moment, you need to pray to the Father through Jesus Christ about your frustrations. The old Saints used to sing a song that was written by Elisha Albright Hoffman (1839-1929), and it said, "I must tell Jesus all of my trials; I cannot bear these burdens alone; In my distress, He kindly will help me; He ever loves and cares for His own. I must tell Jesus! I must tell Jesus! I cannot bear my burdens alone; I must tell Jesus! I must tell Jesus! Jesus can help me, Jesus alone. I do not know if this songwriter was married; however, when she penned these words, she included those married couples. Because sometimes Jesus alone is the only one who can help you through some of the attacks launched against your relationship. Satan cunningly gets you to believe that your spouse is not your ally but your enemy.

It is never a good feeling to disagree or argue, but it's bound to happen when two people try to make one life together. There are articles claiming that it is healthy to disagree in a marriage. When you are genuinely connected to the right mate, you learn to agree. In other words, operating in disagreement is not an option. The Bible teaches in Philippians 2:2, "Fulfil ye my joy, that ye be likeminded, having the same love, being of one accord, of one mind." It takes work to get and keep a marriage afloat and going in the right direction. Married couples seem clueless about their marriage being seriously contested by spiritual forces. The enemy wants marriages not to operate in agreement. He introduces married people to a spirit of selfishness disguised as a desire to maintain individuality. They say things such as, "I can do what I want." "I can have my own opinion and ideas."

I believe a marriage is made up of three people: the man (groom), the woman (bride), and the Holy Spirit (God). These three people represent the God of all Creation from a spiritual perspective. The Godhead is made up of God the Father, God the Son, and God the Holy Spirit. Satan hates this representation in marriage because he considers himself God's enemy. So, the last thing he wants you to do is to operate in unity. He also knows what (Psalm 46:1) says: *"In unity there is strength."*

Chapter 12:
Capping It Off!

I use the expression "capping it off" to bring my thoughts about marriage to an acceptable conclusion. Many of you know it stops the flow when you cap something off. "Capping it off" doesn't mean permanent. Because the cap can be removed, the flow can begin flowing again.

In our Couples Are Partners (CAP), a training module for married couples, we deal with many issues that can develop in marriage. We also share resources and preventative ideas that will positively impact a marriage. So "Capping it off" is a play on CAP, our marriage ministry of the Family Life Missionary Baptist Church. So, here are some final thoughts that my bride and I have shared with couples through this ministry for many years. We believe a strong marital relationship is a marriage built on an intimate partnership between a right-thinking man and woman. This unique friendship is the bedrock that will transition a couple out of a couple being a partner to each other into a vibrantly healthy, committed marriage relationship. Here are some thoughts that will help you better understand the capping-off concept. You need to see your marriage as your greatest investment, create the best quality of life, and engage your marriage into a relationship of oneness.

1. Greatest Investment Ever

Your marriage is probably your next greatest investment outside of having a genuine relationship with Christ. You've put everything in this relationship. You made promises and commitments, believing it would create a fruitful relationship. You sacrificed so-called friends and family to have a strong marriage. You recognized that your marriage was a significant investment.

An investment is something you take very seriously, and if you don't, you should.

Investments will always be geared towards something.

- Money is invested for (something) to earn more money to build or improve (something).
- Time is invested in doing (something) or making (something) better.

All of the investments you've made have this crucial component in them. They will cause you to give something extra, anticipating a more significant outcome. Some of them will have you taking a risk because you believe in your investment. When we consider investing, we think about money and material possessions. However, when you invest, you are committed to putting in everything required for your investment to yield a return. And so it is with your marriage.

Your marriage should reflect the ideal, showing that you put everything you had into it to be successful. You have to see it as your most significant investment. This will allow you to feel emotions and anything else that would keep you from giving your best to your spouse. You will cherish your investment. Picture your marriage as a very expensive diamond ring. Because you value your investment in acquiring this ring, you're willing to take the required steps to maintain its pristine appearance and condition. Yes, you are assured of getting it cleaned regularly. You will have it inspected to ensure that the prongs holding that precious stone in place are not damaged or need to be adjusted. Because you're serious about your investment, you work to ensure it does not lose value.

2. The Best Quality of Life

I mentioned earlier that when times get tough, be quick to forgive and accept forgiveness. Forgiveness is one of the greatest attributes given to humankind. It is smart for married people to use it as often as needed. By doing so, married couples can maintain the love and commitment made in their covenant with each other and the Holy Spirit.

To some degree, every marriage should be working at keeping the love first experienced when getting to know one another. To have a level of commitment that will allow a marriage to work through challenges that will avail themselves as the marriage will require them to be authentic about their love for one another. From a therapeutic perspective, a high-quality marriage can significantly boost your overall quality of life. When compared to being single, marriage offers many benefits, including:

Problem-solving: A marriage involves two people working together to solve problems. This can be a significant advantage over being single, where you are solely responsible for addressing your challenges.

Support: A supportive spouse can provide invaluable emotional and practical support. This can be especially helpful during difficult times.

Companionship: A marriage can provide companionship and intimacy. This can be a significant source of happiness and fulfillment.

To fully harness the advantages of marriage, it's crucial to collaborate effectively as a couple and engage in open, honest communication. When two individuals are aligned in their goals and offer mutual support, they can accomplish significant achievements together. Here are some tips for creating a high-quality marriage:

Make time for each other. Schedule regular date nights or make time to talk and connect daily.

Be supportive of each other's goals and dreams. Encourage your spouse to pursue their passions and be there for them when they need you.

Communicate openly and honestly. Share your thoughts, feelings, and needs with your spouse. Be willing to listen to your spouse's perspective as well.

Resolve conflict in a healthy way. When you disagree with your spouse, try to stay calm and respectful. Avoid personal attacks and name-calling.

Be affectionate and let your spouse know how much you love and appreciate them. Physical touch is a powerful way to connect with your spouse.

If you are struggling in your marriage, consider seeking professional help from a therapist or counselor. They can teach you communication skills and help you resolve any conflicts.

My bride and I wouldn't operate half as well if we didn't have one another looking out for each other. She reminds me to visit the doctor for a check-up and schedule the appointments. I remind her that we need to work out to maintain good health; I consistently go to the gym, which inspires her to do her workout sessions. We are guilty of doing some of the same things related to the food we eat, how we move about in the places we go, and how we look out for one another, qualifying those places to be safe.

I shared these things to give you a snapshot of some of the little things we take for granted. All these things contribute to us having a better quality of life. As a married couple, you should always invest in your spouse. Investing in your spouse in many ways, you are investing in yourself. According to scripture, *"You are no longer twain but one."* Your investment in your marriage clearly indicates that you understand you are one.

3. The Oneness

When one considers oneness, the apparent thought is being alone. However, when it comes to marriage, for some people they must have an epiphany in the marriage journey for God's process to work. This new enlightenment allows them to seek oneness in their marriage relationship. Many examples around you would project marriages that are not operating as one. If you are one of those couples always seeking counseling from other married couples, perhaps you've been counseled by a married couple who have not accepted the one God speaks about in His word.

Mathew 19:6 says, *"Wherefore they are no more twain, but one flesh. What therefore God hath joined together, let not man put asunder."*

Since marriage is God's ideal, referring to His word about marriage is good. So, let's take a brief exegetical journey as we share the essence of this text. **The (A)- clause** says, "Wherefore they are no more twain, but one flesh." Wherefore - "for this reason or cause," "they are no more twain," they are no longer two people; they are now one person. No matter how you look at this, God says He has taken two people and made them one. Don't waste time figuring this out; trust God's words. You may not want to be one. You may be fighting for your individuality and identity. Still, God tells the man and woman to become one in His marriage concept. I believe the oneness allows the marriage to work the way it was designed so that God will ultimately be glorified because of this special union.

In the (B) clause of this verse, God says, "What therefore God hath joined together, let not man put asunder." The Greek word for asunder is χωριστά, and it means separately, apart, or singly. In other words, because God has brought you together and He's making you into one, humankind does not have the authority to separate, break you apart, or come in between the two of you, trying to make you single again. Please take this counseling. If you are talking to people, it doesn't matter if they are married. They are talking against your spouse; you must disallow that conversation and possibly end the relationship. It would help if you did not have unqualified or unjustified voices in your marriage. You may not see your marriage as a divinely inspired covenant between you and God, but God does.

Marriage is serious to God, and He emphasizes what you must do to have the type of marriage you desire but that will bring Him honor. So, in the Old Testament, He says in Genesis 2:24: Therefore, a man shall leave his father and mother and be joined to his wife, and they shall become one flesh.

And for those New Testament readers only, He repeats Himself in Ephesians 5:31, *"For this cause shall a man leave his father and mother, and shall be joined unto his wife, and they two shall be one flesh."*

Appendix

Overseer Assistant Pastor Diane Rodriguez-Burton

Greater Works Baptist Church, Jonesboro, Georgia

I am excited about the book "Put a Cap on It," based on one of the progressive programs from Family Life Missionary Baptist Church. The program is called Capping It Off and was created to highlight the idea that couples are partners. Senior Pastor Bishop Alfred T. Lands is the author of "Put a Cap on It."

Interestingly, the author has laid out prerequisites for having and maintaining successful marriages from a Christian perspective, and he makes the work sound fun. The play on words for the book title was also quite fascinating.

In the book, Bishop Lands tackles the subject of a successful marriage by ensuring that each party, male and female, understands God defines the marriage covenant and each party's role. The book provides models of the appearance couples portray to onlookers, which may or may not reflect a good marriage based on the pattern of the biblical marriage covenant. As stated, man is quick to object to basic scripture suggestions such as, "Will a man leave his mother and father and cleave to his wife wherein doing so they become one flesh. He believes his plan is better until he obeys God's instructions.

The book offers handy instructions that touch on the whole covenant and what can and, in some cases, must be done for the success of the marriage. Some people will view the written pages as a guide for newlyweds or troubled couples. It is more than just a beginner's training manual; it is based on the word of God to help any or all marriages improve. Marriage is defined by God, who established the holy union between His most precious creation within the universe- humanity. The book points out a godly pattern in the word of God as the biblical model, which is the premise for authoring this book.

Alfred T. Lands

The thesis is that a successful marriage requires work, and it depends much more on the couple's attitude in their pursuit to glorify the creator who set the idea of marriage in place in the beginning. Most marriages can use the helpful hints provided. At some point in our marriage, most of us thought that if we tried harder to be nicer to our mates, it would be enough for great success despite bad or mediocre beginnings. According to Bishop Lands and the Word of God, this is not so.

Most of the evidence Bishop Lands gives us about how to have a successful marriage is of personal experience, research from others who appear to have had or are currently living the oneness in a successful marriage, and how the evidence follows the basic tenet of what God the creator and designer of marriage as laid out in His Word. The word of God is truth, and nonfictional information is my favorite reading because it deals with real things. I am a Christian and depend on testimonials of individuals who have experienced success within their covenantal arrangement based on God's pattern for continual encouragement.

The book points out that someone is always watching. The writer says one's marriage is a journey through life. "Many people are watching you as an example, and you may be watching other marriages as you try to understand better what marriage is all about." This life is a natural stage, and how the audience perceives your life affects them, and in some cases, it is profound enough to make a difference in the lives of others. Did you know that the children in your life are the students who occupy the front row seats in your marriage performance? Children learn from their parents, and when they grow up, they usually mimic what they know, which is not always verbal.

This book offers information that will sharpen the reader's skills, leaving them amazed at the rate of Christian progression, which can positively compound marital success as one refers back to it as time goes by. Anyone's marriage can improve when the parties involved desire success as spouses who agree in oneness from a Christian perspective.

There is help in having and enjoying a beautiful and meaningful marital relationship.

This manual is a God-sent guide the Lord has placed on the writer's heart. I encourage anyone currently married or contemplating marriage to get this book. This book provides answers, highlights common misconceptions, and offers improvement skills from scripture and guidance based on Christian-rooted experiences. I am blessed to have been allowed to review such exciting and helpful words of wisdom.

Dr. Author Carson, Jr.

Springfield Missionary Baptist Church, Atlanta, Georgia

CHAPTER 10

1. Seen on purpose? Could this title reflect more about avoiding hypocrisy in marriage?

2. Some marriages do conform to what their parents or some important person's marriage was like.

The negativity might motivate them to be the opposite of what they saw.

3. Growth must take place to have a solid and successful marriage. The view changes away from what others are like and decides to be what they should be.

4. Yes, couples must push past go right past those not-so-good examples of marriage. I think it happens as a couple finds their own place in their own marriage. They know they are bound or limited by what they have seen. They can be better and better than the good example they saw.

CHAPTER 11

1. The title is very striking and suggests that maintaining will allow one to see the gains they have made.

2. The couple must be intentional about marriage. They must say we are going to make this work. We are going to hold on to each other when(if) it gets tough.

3. There are keys to a successful marriage, and one key is intentionality.

4. One must be intentional with everything they do, including being kind.

5. The little things especially matter.

6. This is an excellent point for learning to agree; this is intentional.

7. Being intentional about who the person is, their likes and dislikes

8. New things and discoveries come with longevity and maturity.

9. Marriage is always a work in progress, always becoming.

10. Staying in touch with each other brings a closer connection.

11. The idea of a developing marriage is important because it leads to unity in the marriage.

CHAPTER 12

1. Marriage as an investment is pointed out because it is.

2. We should look for our return each year like we do with financial investments.

3. Each year brings about a higher quality of life, regardless of the struggles.

4. The point is that our investment in our marriage is an investment in a person but an investment in who we are and speaks to our willingness to make the best marriage possible.

5. Our investment will produce oneness because we have skin in the game.

CLOSING THOUGHTS

Thanks for the opportunity to share my reflections on this wonderful piece of work that will bless many who read it and put into practice the principles set forth in it. The principles set forth are biblical. They conform to what God has said about marriage. This book fosters the idea mentioned in the closing from Ephesians 5:31. This is God's purpose and place for marriage that a man and a woman, nothing else, a man and a woman would become one flesh.

Archbishop Dr. Sterling Lands II

Greater Calvary Bible Church and Family Life International Fellowship, Inc., Austin, Texas

Chapter 10:

The Display

This chapter gave me cause to pause and consider the rudiments of the marriage relationship. Often engaged and soon married individuals work overtime to keep their "look-good looking-good." As this chapter points out, this effort eventually follows the rules of diminishing returns. Once you become used to the value of the relationship, if not reminded of that value on a regular basis, the original value diminishes. Couples often move through the cycle of productive returns to diminishing returns to negative returns to the demise of the relationship. The lack of a clear biblical understanding that God made man and woman unique, uniquely different. Every effort to reverse the diminishing returns follows the cycle of "use-misuse-abuse" to the detriment of the relationship. "For many, marriage is a daunting quest journey with no clear path and a fight with no clear winner." As a result, observers get mis-messages that result in misdirection's for future relationships.

Chapter 11:

Gaining While Maintaining

This is a great chapter because it highlights the very foundation's definition and purpose. Building a God-honoring marriage relationship becomes progressively axiomatic when one's definition and purpose are clear. Every couple can use biblical principles to position themselves within their relationships, leading to valuable stability in their marriage.

Chapter 12:

Capping It Off!

The expression "capping it off" sums up the biblical process of growth and development in marriage. I am excited about this "New Work" because the principles are tried and true. The Ministry at the Family Life Missionary Baptist Church has presented and still provides a laboratory for developing and maintaining successful biblical marriage in the midst of unprecedented attacks against marriage. This book should be used as a stabilizing tool for marriages everywhere.

Blessings, +++Dr. Sterling Lands II.

Pastor Darien, Sr., and Minister Shakiera Brooks

Servants in the Body of Christ and faithful servants in the Family Life Missionary Baptist Church

"Put a CAP on it" by Bishop Alfred T. Lands is an exceptional book that delves deep into the intricacies of marriage. By drawing a parallel between various art concepts and different aspects of marriage, Bishop Lands makes some profound points that empower married couples and single people alike with a greater understanding of the fundamental factors of a successful marriage. He helps us realize the importance of acknowledging our differences to create a harmonious union. The analogy of complementary colors creating something amazing when brought together is a powerful metaphor for the potential of marriage between two unique individuals. Bishop Lands also provides insights into the gravity of leaving one's family to form a bond with a virtual stranger. This concept alone is quite powerful as it provides a perspective that counters the normal mindset and sets the tone for the understanding that God is necessary for marriage to work. It's a perspective that truly emphasizes the need to approach marriage with care and respect for the institution. Furthermore, Bishop Lands reminds us that our actions within a marriage are always on display, whether we realize it or not. Therefore, we must model our marriage as an example that we're proud of and that aligns with God's divine design of marriage.

Bishop Lands also helps us understand marriage as a journey on which you must continuously learn and relearn your spouse as you both evolve over time. Understanding and adapting to these changes is crucial for a strong, enduring relationship. He also highlights the importance of setting your own pace in marriage and recognizing that every marriage is unique. This is significant in a culture where a couple's goals are usually dictated by false perceptions displayed in the media. Another powerful takeaway is the idea of investing in your marriage, much like we invest in various aspects of our lives, to foster a fulfilling and rewarding partnership. The emphasis on kindness, rather than niceness, as an expression of love and grace that is essential for marital success was also powerful. Bishop's thought-provoking analogy of marriage to the Holy Trinity stresses that marriage should include God as an integral part of the union, and extension of grace is a tangible way to accomplish this. The book's conclusion emphasizes the oneness of marriage, the idea that two individuals become one. This oneness is a beautiful representation of the union God intended for marriage, highlighting the importance of keeping divisive elements away from this sacred bond. In conclusion, "Put a CAP on it" provides profound insights into marriage, offering valuable advice and perspectives that can help couples navigate the complexities of this lifelong journey. As we approach 14 years of marriage under the guidance and support of Bishop Alfred T. Lands and the Couples Are Partners experience, we attribute our marital success to learning, understanding, and applying the concepts presented in this book. It's a must-read for anyone seeking a deeper understanding of the institution of marriage and the keys to a successful and fulfilling partnership.

Dr. William E. Flippin

The Greater Piney Grove Baptist Church, Atlanta, Georgia

From day one, when I met Bishop Alfred Lands, it was clear that one of his gifts was to teach and model a God-called family. He successfully formed a Sunday Church School class at our church thirty years ago centered around family unity and how to maintain cohesiveness. Thus, he has never wavered. He says in this book that we must be keenly aware that other couples are watching the example we demonstrate in our marriages. Next year marks fifty years since I have had the joy of being a husband to my wife.

A few weeks ago, I preached about "Lessons at The Potters House". The prophet Jeremiah gets a message from the Lord, Jeremiah, "Arise, and go down to the potter's house, and there I will cause thee to hear my words." Note that not one word was exchanged. Bishop Lands stresses this point throughout his work. Never minimize the fact that many lessons can be learned by observation.

This is a must read for any person or church interested in leading groups on marriage. If you will use his work, we all can ***"CAP IT OFF."***

Deacon-elect Thomas and Deaconess Trunae A. Green

Servants in the Body of Christ and faithful servants in the Family Life Missionary Baptist Church

Alfred T. Lands

*In Chapter 10, "The Display," Bishop Lands refers to Claude Monet's Complementary Color Scheme, which suggests that colors on the opposite sides of the color wheel complement one another. This reminds me of 2 Corinthians 12:9 [9] **But he said to me, "My grace is sufficient for you, for my power is made perfect in weakness." Therefore, I will boast all the more gladly about my weaknesses, so that Christ's power may rest on me.** Marriage is a Godly construct. As a husband and wife, we have experienced God's work through each other to stand up in areas where we are weak. This chapter reminds us that we must intentionally invest in our marriage, honor our vows, and honor the Holy Spirit's presence so that our marriage glorifies God and blesses those who are watching.*

The chapter titled "Gaining While Maintaining" served as a road map and "How to" manual regarding how to progress in marriage. Although we have been married ten years, at times, it still feels like we are newlyweds. The premise of this chapter spoke directly to our marriage and helped us to align our pace and run our race. My bride and I often consider the changes we've both undergone in the duration of our marriage. Some have been subtle, while others have been massive. This dynamic illustrates the importance of marital development, as mentioned in chapter 11. While we must be honest that things are very different from when we first got married, we are so excited to grow and develop together as one and to experience what God will do with our marriage in the future. "Kindness…it is a movement that can be triggered by a person acting on purpose." This is a profound statement that has helped us to change our approach and perspective on marriage.

The conclusive thoughts in the final chapter, "Capping It Off," were like a launching pad in our marriage! Little investment, little reward. Great investment, Great reward! This is a key takeaway from this chapter. We desire to return a great yield from our marriage, including glorifying God, pleasing one another, and setting a great example of marriage before our children. This book is an invaluable investment in our marriage; we are already noticing a greater quality of life, greater friendship, and more joy!

A Brief Look at the Author

Pastor Alfred Trunell Lands and his bride, Executive Pastor Bishop Rosemary, are the esteemed Founder and Pastor of the Family Life Missionary Baptist Church, where God's vision for families comes to life. Pastor Lands was born in New Orleans and grew up in Baton Rouge, Louisiana. His academic journey includes a Bachelor of Fine Arts from the University of Southwestern Louisiana, a Master of Urban Ministry from the Urban Seminary of Atlanta, and a Master of Divinity from Jehovah Jireh Bible Institute of Higher Learning. He is currently pursuing a Doctoral degree in Theology at Metropolitan University.

Pastor Lands and his bride, Bishop Rosemary, have faithfully served youth and families throughout their ministry. His journey into ministry began with licensure to preach at New Calvary Missionary Baptist Church in Atlanta, Georgia, under the leadership of the late Pastor P.L. Redmond, Jr. He was later ordained into the Gospel Ministry at Greater Piney Grove Baptist Church, under the guidance of Dr. William E. Flippin. In his commitment to the ministry of Family Affairs, he was appointed Overseer in The Lord's Churches Fellowships and Ministries International, Inc. Later, The Family Life International Fellowship, Inc. consecrated him as a Bishop. Pastor Lands is an esteemed member of the "House of Bishops," Master's Circle Christian Fellowship, and the Evangelical Episcopal Communion. He is also a founding member and former Moderator of the S.A.B.A. (Statewide Association of Baptist Assemblies), a historic association of predominantly black Pastors within the Georgia Baptist Convention, serving the Southwest Atlanta area.

Pastor Lands, apart from his role as a religious leader, serves as the founder and president of TruFaith Music, LLC, a record label associated with the Family Life Missionary Baptist Church. The label's main artist is "The Family," a diverse group of gospel artists that includes God's Gurls, an all-female band; Gospel Rappers Rev. Taj B. & B'Lat; The Heavenly H.O.R.N.S.; and the legendary "Vocalist Warrior" Rev. Darien Brooks.

Passionate about strengthening families and addressing community issues, Pastor Lands and his bride founded Love Involves Family Everyday, Inc., a ministry dedicated to holistic family empowerment. He and his bride have also hosted a marriage-focused segment called "Taking the Family to Godly Heights" on KISS 104.1 FM. Their radio journey also includes a show called "The Bishop and His Bride," they are currently developing a podcast with the same name. Additionally, Pastor Lands leads a ministry called "Just Man Talk," providing a platform for men to discuss community matters with community leaders and fellow men.

Alongside his pastoral and ministry responsibilities, Pastor Lands and his bride have successfully operated their graphic design business, Alfred Lands Creative Design Solutions, for over 35 years. Their two gifted children have formed an all-female Gospel band, God's Gurls. Deaconess Trunae' Alyse Green, who plays lead guitar, is married to Deacon-elect Thomas Green, and they are blessed with three children: Tylan Trunell, Tory Leon, and Tyla Tru Green. The youngest, Deaconess-elect Trulyse Faith Lands, is an accomplished bass guitarist.

Pastor Lands and his bride have also played a pivotal role in raising two nephews, Pastor Taj B. Lands, originally from Los Angeles, California, and Pastor Darien Brooks, a native of Milwaukee, Wisconsin. Pastor Brooks is happily married to Minister Shakiera Brooks, and they are the proud parents of four sons and a daughter: Darien Jr., Donovon, Destin, Dasia, and Dawson. The Lands family is an inspiring example of unwavering faith, dedication to education, and active involvement in their church and community. Their lives exemplify a commitment to God-centered living and the importance of strong family relationships.

Printed by Libri Plureos GmbH in Hamburg, Germany